BOYZONE

A Key to Our Life

EUGENE MASTERSON

EDINBURGH AND LONDON

EUGENE MASTERSON is the music correspondent for the *Star* in Dublin. He is also the Irish correspondent for *Melody Maker*. He has travelled all over the world, interviewing acts such as U2, Take That, REM, INXS and Diana Ross. He was the first Irish national newspaper journalist to interview the Cranberries, the Sawdoctors, Therapy? and the Commitments' Andrew Strong, and the first to write about Boyzone.

The photograph of Ronan with his family on page 17 appears courtesy of Kieran Corrigan
The portfolio photographs of the band appear courtesy of Kip Carroll, WAR management

First published in Great Britain in 1995 by
MAINSTREAM PUBLISHING COMPANY (EDINBURGH) LTD
7 Albany Street
Edinburgh EH1 3UG

Reprinted 1995, 1996 (twice)

ISBN 1 85158 768 3

A catalogue record for this book is available from the British Library

Designed by Janene Reid

Printed and bound in Great Britain by Butler and Tanner Ltd, Frome

Contents

INTRODUCTION

In November 1993 I received a phone-call from a young lad who wanted to join a pop group being formed in Dublin. He was eager to know who he should apply to for an audition and whether I could give him a contact number. The lad who called was Steve Gately, now adorning the walls of tens of thousands of teenagers.

Boyzone with Eugene Masterson at the IRMA Irish Music Industry Awards, April 1995

Steve, Ronan, Shane, Keith and Mikey are members of the biggest ever pop phenomenon to come out of Ireland. We might have everything from the likes of U2, the Cranberries and Sinead O'Connor to Enya and Chris de Burgh, but Ireland has never produced a real pop band. Three of them are still only teenagers.

I attended Boyzone's formation at their last audition in Dublin, and then, a little over a year later at the *Smash Hits* Poll Winners' awards in London, I had the pleasure of being first to tell them that they had entered the UK charts at No. 10 with 'Love Me For a Reason'.

Boyzone and their fans have one man to thank for their formation: Louis Walsh, the man who thought up the idea and had the guts to go for it. The band has now sold over 600,000 copies of 'Love Me For a Reason' in the UK, a record for a debut release by an Irish act. And it's not just Irish and British kids who are lapping up Boyzone – they've now become a commodity much in demand throughout Europe. Perhaps they can even break America, something Take That have still to do.

This book may seem simple in its approach but it took a hell of a lot of time and work, and the reason it works is that it's exactly what Boyzone's fans want.

Eugene Masterson
Dublin, April 1995

SHANE
LYNCH

Family

I was born in the Coombe Hospital in Dublin on 3 July 1976, and I have lived in Donaghmede all my life.

I am the only boy in my family, and I have five sisters. The oldest in my family is Tara, who's 23. She's a choreographer with her own dance troupe in Baldoyle, which is nearby. She helped me out in the early days with routines and dance steps. Then there's Alison. She's 20, and she used to go out with Keith from Boyzone before we were in the band. It's a major coincidence. Alison was once an All-Ireland champion gymnast. Next are the twins, Keavy and Edele, who are 16. They're still at school and sometimes get pestered for autographs by the girls there. Naomi is the youngest, at 11. She loves me being in the band and has posters of us all over her bedroom.

My Dad, Brendan, is a mechanic. He owns a garage in Finglas, where I used to work with him. I've always looked up to him since I was young, and he's a bit of a hero to me. I have a pretty close bond with my Dad, partly because he raced cars and can fix them. He used to do a lot of stock-car racing and worked on hot-rods. He would have loved to get involved in Formula 1, but because he had us kids it was too dangerous. My Mum's name is Noleen. She's what you would call nowadays a homemaker. She's very supportive of me and I've always got on great with her.

I didn't find it a problem growing up in a houseful of girls – I used to be out with my mates most of the time anyway. I used to tease the girls a lot and play tricks on them. I

Shane was a car freak even at the age of one and a half

By the age of eight he was trying out tricks on his bike

love practical jokes. Once when we were on holiday in Galway, me and my sisters played with a ouija board. It worked. We were talking to a girl called Sam. We were pretty amazed when we got through to somebody from the after-life. Then she said that I was evil and that my sisters had to kill me. I was very shocked. But then they asked if it was the Shane that was in the room that they had to kill. When she said no, I was pretty relieved.

The whole family used to go abroad on holiday every year. I've been to Portugal 13 times! I used to be nearly fluent in Portuguese but I haven't a clue any more. The scariest moment of my life happened on holiday in Portugal. I was with my two cousins, Brian and Colm, and we got stranded on a secluded beach after the tide started coming in. I'm a pretty good swimmer, and two of us were able to swim away, while the third guy was eventually picked up by a fishing boat. It was a close shave.

I have a pet snake called Caesar. I got it in a pet shop in Georges Street in Dublin for about £150. It's a three-foot garter snake. My Mum, who is scared to death of snakes, didn't realise I was keeping it in a box at the bottom of my wardrobe, but I was secretly feeding it on gold-fish all the time. When I'm away on tour, I get my sister, Alison, to feed it. My Mum has found out about it but she doesn't mind as long as I keep it away from her.

I have been dying my hair black since I was 15. Black is my favourite colour. The real colour of my hair is brown. Last year I tried a style called sticks, which involves wrapping hair extensions around small plaits. It took eight hours to do in Lunatic Fringe hairdressers in Grafton Street in Dublin. It cost me £150. You can see it in a lot of our earlier publicity shots, and I liked it a lot. It then started to go shaggy after a while, and I eventually washed it out. I might get it done again but it was so expensive that I might just style it myself.

For the past year and a half I have been shaving my right eyebrow in the middle. I like it as an image. I'm now thinking of having electrolysis done on it so it won't grow back, as I'm tired of plucking it all the time.

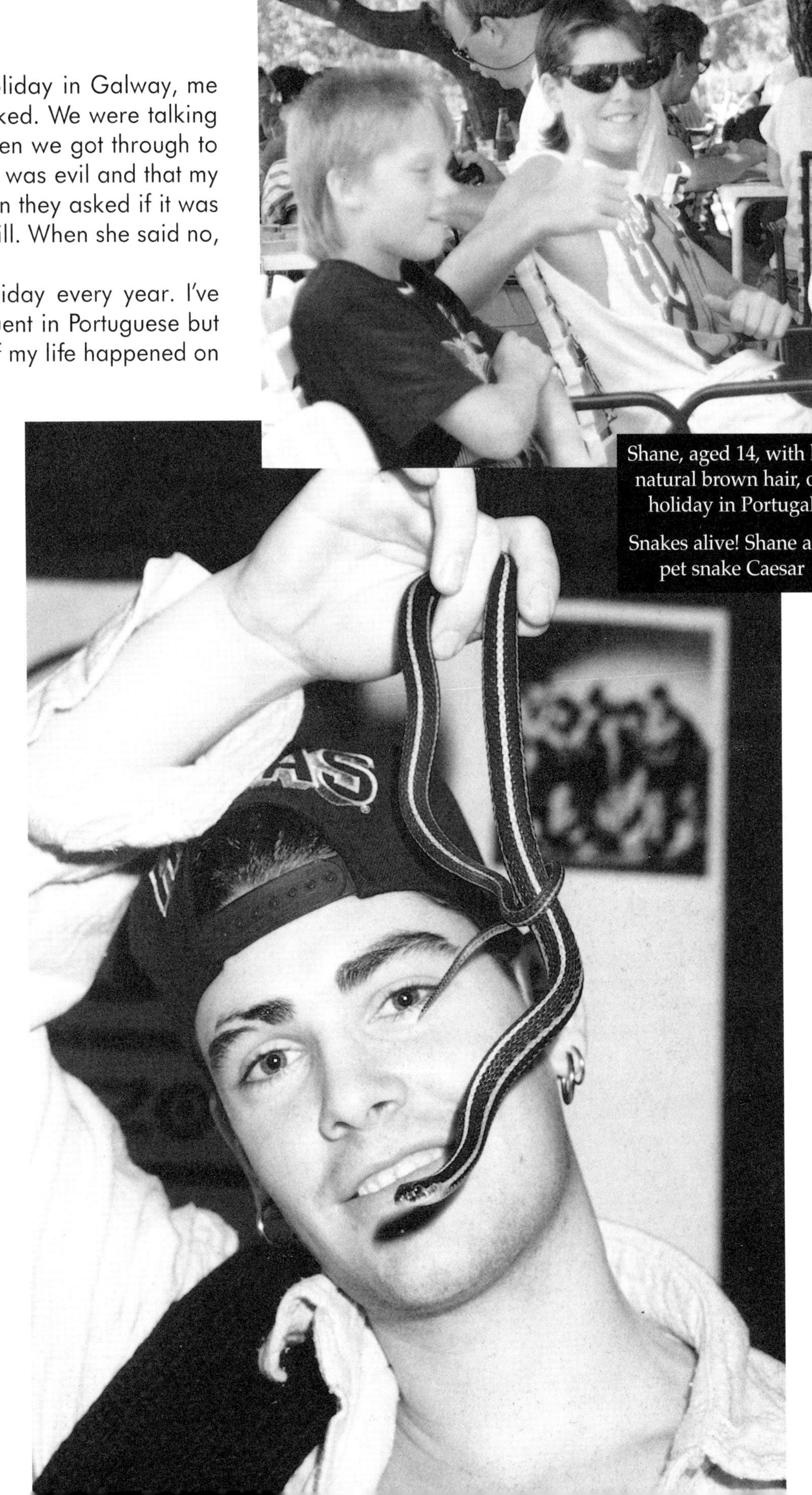

Shane, aged 14, with his natural brown hair, on holiday in Portugal

Snakes alive! Shane and pet snake Caesar

School

We are the champions! Shane, aged 9, after winning a swimming gala with friends

Shane, aged 14

I can barely remember my first day in school – I just remember crying. It was an all boys' school called St Brigid's, which is in Killester. I enjoyed art and PE, and I sang in a choir in school and also in Killester Church.

I went with the flow, and I didn't bully or get bullied. I did high-jumping and long-jumping in primary school. I won plenty of medals, as I was very good at the high-jump and was a good runner. I was also pretty good at swimming and won a few competitions.

At the Dublin Schools Athletics Championships in Santry Stadium I won a gold medal when I was about eight for the high-jump and I won a prize for best all-round athlete. They were pretty pleased at school.

I only got caught mitching once, and that was in primary school. I went off with a friend but he ratted on me and he wasn't a friend any more. He couldn't get a note to say he was sick and I could, but I got found out when he said that he was with me. We went into town and hung about the Ilac Shopping Centre. I was about ten and I can't remember the punishment. My Mum and Dad were annoyed because they didn't expect it of me, as I had never done anything wrong before.

Going to secondary school was a big change. I went to Grange Community College. I had to move from an all boys' school to a mixed school, which I had to get used to. I was interested only in motorbikes, and I was very nervous with girls. The first friend I made in secondary school was a guy called Carl Melhorn. The reason I made friends with him was that I was sitting with him in French class, the very first class we had, and we just had a good laugh. I never really made friends with the girls, not in my class anyway.

The teachers thought I was quite a nice lad. I never gave trouble – I simply never did anything. My favourite teacher in secondary school was a guy called Dinny Ryan, who used to teach Irish (Gaelic). I hated Irish and didn't have a clue about it until I got into his class. He was just a brilliant teacher. He was such a messer himself that I liked learning it, but when he got serious you'd have to keep your head down.

I had a crush on my history teacher, Miss Ryan. She was very strongly feminist, and I think that's what I liked about her. She was quite small, with blonde hair. Although she wasn't an amazing-looking woman, I just found something attractive about her. As a teacher, she was very strict, and, of course, I never made it known that I fancied her.

I stayed at the school for three years and did my Junior Certificate. I got three honours and five passes. I didn't give a damn about my exams. I did all the sports days at school but once I got into third year I really had no interest in school and used to go out on the bonk (play truant) with Derek Kane and Simon Fowley. Along with Francis Murphy, they're still my best mates. We just used go out and mess around with our motorbikes.

I had an early curfew. I wasn't allowed to stay out late, but I couldn't have asked for a better childhood – it was brilliant.

After the Junior Certificate, I was told by one of the teachers not to go back to school. I got into trouble for swearing in an English class and was sent out of the room. One of the teachers came walking by and stopped and said to me, 'Now, Mr Lynch, I don't think you should come back next term after your Junior Certificate.'

I said, 'Why not? I didn't do anything.'

He said, 'Precisely the point, you don't do anything. All you do is pose around the school.'

As far as I was concerned, I wasn't posing around the school, but the teachers seemed to think so. I never told my folks. When I went home, all I said was that I wanted to leave school.

Around that time, I started drinking but it was just a couple of cans now and again at a friend's house. My father found out about it and then I lost interest in it. It was just an exciting thing to do.

I've never had any interest in drugs. I was at a disco last year, and I couldn't believe the number of people there who I grew up with and who I knew were on Ecstasy. I think drugs are disgraceful and people who take them are sad.

No one measures up to Shane

Bikes and Cars

I always had an interest in motorbikes and cars, and it was a bonus having a father who was a mechanic and owned a garage. I got into bikes because my Dad used to race them. Then I started messing around with them, and when I left school I became a mechanic. I got my first bike when I was really young, about three, and I also got my first toy car around that time. I got my first BMX when I was eight, and then I started racing them. I won the All-Ireland Championships when I was 14, and I also won the Portuguese Championships.

When Derek got a motorbike, I started messing around with that, and then my Dad gave me his Yamaha when I was 14. I didn't ride my motorbike on the roads, as I was too young. I used to push it down the road to the fields near where I live in Donaghmede and ride around there. I took to it naturally but I had a few falls, of course. I stuck with the Yamaha and I'm now waiting for a new bike. I hate Harley Davidson bikes – I'd like an off-road bike or else a really good road bike, like a ZZR or something like that. My first car was a four-by-four jeep, which I bought when I turned 17 and which I still drive. I entered a rally in Galway later that year – I love rallying. Later, I bought a Golf GTI but I wrote that off one night early last year after Keith and I had left his house following a practice session with the band. I was going too fast, at over 100 mph. We were lucky to escape with our lives when it crashed through a ditch and somersaulted a few times.

I love speed. The car I have now, a twin-cam Corolla, can do up to 140 or 150 mph. I once did 135 mph in it but ran out of road. I was coming home from Arklow with Derek after I had bought a new set of wheels. I'm surprised I haven't been locked up yet. I've been done a few times for tax and dangerous driving, although I've never been in court yet.

Shane wins a BMX championship at the age of 11

BMX maniac Shane gets airborne

Work

I started to work part time at my Dad's garage when I was 14. I'd come home from school and work nights, and then I asked him for an apprenticeship. I think he respected me for my decision to leave school because he knew I hated it. I think he was delighted because I wanted to follow in his footsteps.

I started working full time at the end of the summer when I turned 16. I remember walking in and not knowing what to do or where to start. I hadn't a clue, and I stuck out like a sore thumb. There were three mechanics there, and one of the lads, the main man, whose name was Joe but whose nickname was Noddy, showed me the ropes and how to manage things.

I used to go with my Dad to the garage every morning and come back each evening, and he was always asking me questions. It was like being back at school. I was on a proper wage when I started. It was £50 a week, which may not seem like a lot but it wasn't bad for a kid starting off. I was a very good saver, and saved mainly for new parts for my bike.

Shane, aged 16, on holiday in Portugal

HOW WE MET

My interest in music started when I was 12, and the first record I bought was by NWA. I bought it because there was a lot of bad language on it, and, at that age, I thought it was great. I used to listen to the lyrics about the black slums and the Bronx. I was really into it, and it had a really good beat to it. I still love rap music – Public Enemy is my favourite band. I never got involved with bands, as I was quite down to earth. I didn't think of being a pop star.

I did some modelling on the cat-walks and a few photoshoots, but that was my only involvement with the entertainment world. I used to sing in my Dad's garage, and he kept telling me to go for it. So I did. I remember looking at posters of New Kids on the Block when I was about 11 or 12 and saying to myself that someday I'd like to be like them.

I also used to think about the girls having my picture on their walls and fancying me. But there's more to it than that: I can sing too. I had just watched some pop awards on television, and I didn't think I was meant to be a mechanic, so I said to myself, why not have a go?

Me and a guy called Mark got the name of a guy who might be interested in what we were trying to do from a guy in Tops of the Town (an amateur variety competition). Mark had been doing auditions for it, so I was in the right

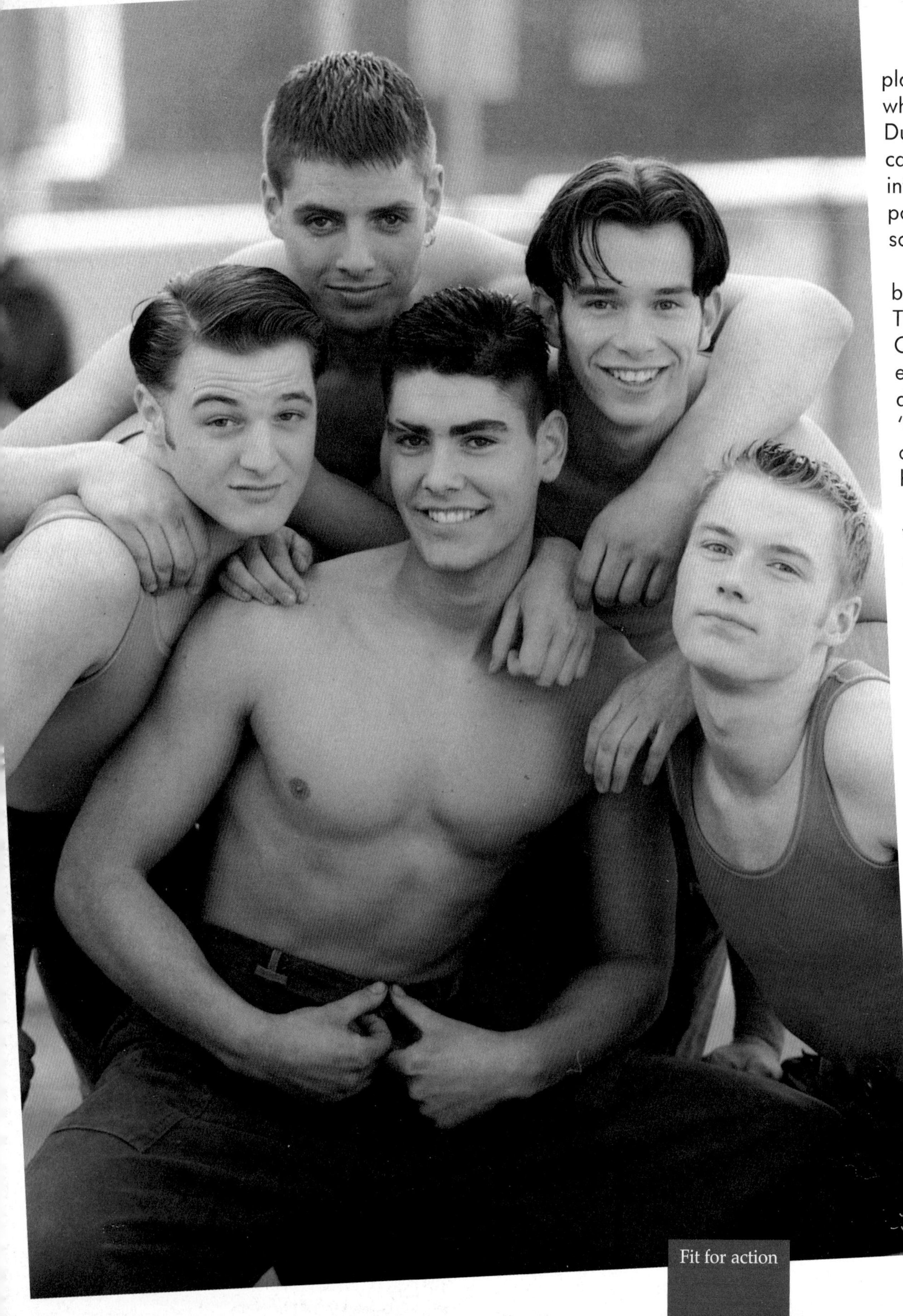

Fit for action

place at the right time. The guy whose name we were given was a Dublin music promoter and agent called Louis Walsh. He was very interested in the idea of forming a pop band and decided to hold some auditions.

I kind of knew I was in the band but I did the auditions anyway. That was in November 1993 at the Ormond Centre in Dublin. Like everybody else, I sang and danced. We all had to do 'Careless Whisper'. I just did the one audition but most of the lads had to do three.

Mark and I were chosen, as were Steve, Keith and Ronan, and a guy called Richard, or Rocky, who is the son of the Irish singer Dickie Rock. Mark and Richard left a few months later, and Mikey was brought in.

I thought it might get big but not like this. I now love being out on tour. It's the best life you could have.

Winning the award for Best New Act at the *Smash Hits* Poll Winners' Awards at the Docklands Arena in London was unreal. Feeling the energy coming from 20,000 screaming fans was unforgettable. We found out later that day that we had just entered the UK charts at No. 10 with 'Love Me For a Reason', and we were delighted with ourselves.

I would like to end up with a lot of money and to see the rest of the lads doing well too. If I make enough, I'll never have to go back to being just a plain mechanic.

RONAN
KEATING

Family

Four-month-old Ronan with sister Linda and brother Gerard

Ronan, aged two, is dwarfed by a wall

I was born at home in Bayside, Dublin, on 3 March 1977. I recently celebrated my 18th birthday. I'm the youngest in my family, and next to me is my brother, Gary, who's 22. He's studying foreign trade at Westchester College in New York. I went over for his 21st birthday party, and I liked the place a lot. Then there's Gerard, 25, who's on Wall Street at the Stock Exchange. He's been there five years. My sister Linda, 27, owns a restaurant in New York. I probably would have ended up working there if I had not joined Boyzone after leaving school. Linda lives in Queens and my two brothers live in upstate New York. If the band hadn't worked out, I think I would have taken up the offer of an athletics scholarship in America because there's nothing in this country. Then there's Ciaran, who's 29 and married to Ann Marie. He's a mechanic and they live in Castleknock in Dublin. They have a son, Conall, who's a year-and-a-half old. I felt very honoured when Ciaran asked me to be his godfather.

My Mum, Marie, used to own a hairdressing salon, and she still does hairdressing. My Dad, Gerry, works for a bottling company. Mum was a bit wary at first when I was getting into Boyzone, but she's now delighted.

I was very close to Gary growing up – I kind of grew up with him. It was hard enough when Gerard left but when Gary left it was terrible. I was very lonely but I had to cope; I had to grow up very quickly.

I remember when I was six or seven hitting my Dad on his face just under his eye with a golf club as I was trying to swing. He had to be taken to hospital to get some stitches. Once when we were on holiday in Killarney, when I was around the same age, I tried my hand at showjumping. Me and Gerard were on the horse, but I made both of us fall off, which was a bit embarrassing, as everyone was laughing.

We moved from Bayside to Dunsany, Co. Meath, just outside Dunshaughlin, when I was about 13. Leaving Bayside was a big move, as I had lived there for so long. I went to school in Sutton, and that's where I made a lot of my friends. My Mam wanted to move to the country but we found it very hard living there. I loved Dublin. Eventually, we moved back, and I now live in Swords, which is about the right distance from the city centre.

A lot of my friends are in college but one really good friend, Stuart McCarron, went to America for six months to work. He's home at the moment, but he's going to go back, and I'll miss him. My other best friend, Mark Maher, is repeating his Leaving Certificate. He was my best friend in Dunshaughlin.

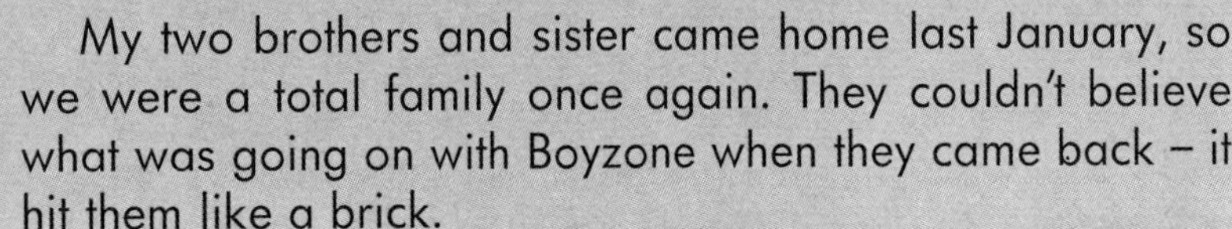

My two brothers and sister came home last January, so we were a total family once again. They couldn't believe what was going on with Boyzone when they came back – it hit them like a brick.

The day I was 17 I got my first driving licence, and it gave me a lot of independence. I had been practising my driving on the local beach for three or four years. I now drive my mother's car, a Vauxhall Astra, which means I don't have to take buses any more. I'm soon going to get a new car of my own, probably a Renault 19. I like go-karting a lot and I recently bought a Scalectrix set.

I think if I did leave home my Mum would be very lonely. She would be very upset because I'm the baby of the family. It's hard enough going away and leaving her for a few weeks.

Ronan, aged two, with snow-white hair, in a family picture

Ronan on his 18th birthday in Swords with his godson, Conall, and parents, Marie and Gerry

School

Four-year-old Ronan about to leave home in Bayside with his brothers, Gerard and Gary, for his first day at school

Ronan, aged 12, on his Confirmation day

I can't remember my first day at school, but I'm told I cried a lot. My first teacher, Miss Cunneen, was a very nice lady and I'd love to meet her again. The school, Bayside Primary School, was mixed. I remember Miss Moran was my next teacher, and then I had Mr Cronin – I got on very well with him. I had Mr Cronin for two years, for fifth and sixth class. We had each teacher for two years. I was older so I got on well with him. I was very good at English and I liked history and PE.

We did a number of plays, including *Cinderella*. I directed one of them, *Rumpelstiltskin*. I was so interested in English that I volunteered to direct the play – that was in sixth class. We usually did nativity plays at Christmas. I played Joseph one year, and I can also remember playing the part of the donkey! I also did a few productions at the nearby Bayside Youth Club.

I was in the local youth club and the cubs and scouts. I did karate, but I never really stayed at anything much for too long. I was never bullied at school – I was always able to look after myself.

It wasn't until secondary school that I got into fights. It was very strange to go to St Fintan's in Sutton, which is an all boys' school run by the Christian Brothers, but I soon got used to it. In first year I remember our music class but I never paid much attention to it as it was always used for choir practice.

I had to come to terms with leaving Bayside and the school in Sutton. I've completely lost touch with my best friend there, John Waldron, who was also my next-door neighbour, as they've moved house, which is very sad. I wouldn't mind meeting him again.

When I moved to my new school in Co. Meath I had a lot of problems. Some of the boys had a chip on their shoulder because I was from Dublin – they didn't like the Dubs. They kind of ganged up on me but I sorted them out. They started on me in the first week at school. They came up and pushed me around, but I said, 'I'm not taking any of this, I'll see you at four o'clock in the schoolyard.' They said something about girls too.

So at four o'clock it was *bang! bang!* I can't remember his name. That was my first big fight, although I was also in a number before I went there, but you know how things are when you're young. After the fight in Meath they left me alone. The school was Dunshaughlin Community College. The teachers also seemed to be biased against me – I didn't get on with any of them. I think that was because I was from Dublin, and they thought I was a bit of an upstart.

My brother, Gary, stayed on at St Fintan's because they didn't want to move him, so I had to go to the new school on my own. My parents didn't get involved in any problems I had with the pupils or teachers at school as it was my business and I wanted to deal with it myself. I was never good at school anyway.

I was there for three years, from the age of 13, and I was very involved in athletics. The distances I did were 200m, 400m and 800m when I was 13. I was in the Dunshaughlin Athletics Club and won a lot of competitions. I won the All-Ireland Championships and I also came second in the Triple A Championships, involving Ireland, England and Wales. I was offered an athletics scholarship to Iona College in upstate New York. My brother, Gerard, had taken up the same scholarship a few years earlier, but I really hadn't got the same determination to become a dedicated athlete.

It was great to get back to St Fintan's, because I knew a lot of the boys there. Even though I had been away for three years, I used to go back to Dublin a lot, so I never really lost touch. I did my Junior Certificate there and got three honours and six passes, which wasn't too good.

I told the careers-guidance teacher that I wanted to do a course in security studies at Mountjoy as I wanted to become a Garda. My grandfather was a Guard and so was my uncle. It was just something that I always wanted to do. I could be in Templemore (the Irish police training academy) now if I wasn't in Boyzone – now that would be scary stuff!

I left school in January 1994. My mother didn't want me to leave and neither did my father. They didn't know what I was getting into. I didn't really persuade them, I just did it. I had to take my own life in my hands.

No. 1 at the age of 13. Ronan wins an Under-14 All-Ireland running title

Ronan surrounded at an autograph-signing session at a Dublin school

Work

I worked part time in shoe shops for four years, first in Simon Hart and then in Korky's. I used to earn about £3 an hour. I remember getting my first wage-packet when I was about 15 and going out with the lads to the Zoo Bar. I didn't spend all of it as I only started drinking recently. I'm not really one for drinking – anyone will tell you that I'm gone after two pints!

I also helped my Mum out in her salon in Dunshaughlin when we lived there. Sometimes I'd give my Dad a hand with his truck, and we travelled all over the country, to Galway and Kerry, which I liked a lot.

When I left school I went back to Korky's for a few weeks while the band was getting on its feet.

On the set of the video for 'Love Me For a Reason' in the Pod nightclub

HOW WE MET

I was always interested in music and writing songs. My favourite singers are George Michael and Sting. I started writing songs in my first year in secondary school in English classes. I never really learned chords, but I had the melodies in my head and I played a bit of guitar. I started out on my brother's guitar.

I joined my first band when I was about 15 and living in Dunshaughlin. All the lads were from there, and I was the lead singer. It was a rock band, and we were into 'Johnny B. Goode' and Nirvana.

My first band had no name – we were really just doing a bit of jamming – but my second band was called Nameste. There was Ian on drums, Stuey on bass, Gordon was on rhythm, Adrian played lead guitar and John was on sax. I was the singer. We won £1,000 in a talent contest at Dorey's pub in Dunshaughlin. We did Chuck Berry's 'Johnny B. Goode' and then 'Ride On' by Christy Moore.

My friend Niall O'Neill told me about the auditions for Boyzone, and I saw a piece in the paper. I thought I'd go for it because I had always admired Take That and I thought that this new band could be as big as them.

The auditions were nerve-wracking. I never thought I'd get it. I remember all the lads from the auditions – Shane, Keith, Mikey and Steve. I actually got talking to Steve. My friend Mark Maher came along with me, but he didn't go for it. We just sat on our own and watched what was happening.

I had to sing George Michael's 'Careless Whisper'. There were three auditions altogether. I also had to dance to Right Said Fred's 'I'm Too Sexy'. I then sang Cat Stevens' 'Father and Son'.

This went on for several days, and I couldn't believe it when they told me at the final audition that I was in the band. We went on the *Late Late Show* the day after we were picked. We had no routine, no choreographer, and we weren't even friends. We were pathetic! We made eejits of ourselves when we danced to Clubhouse's 'Burn, Baby, Burn'.

We signed the Boyzone deal, which was a big decision in our lives, early last year. We have signed away a big part of our lives, but it's what we have all always wanted to do, so we're happy.

We released 'Working My Way Back To You' in Ireland on 26 May last year. It entered the chart at No. 2 and stayed there. We were happy enough that it only got that high, as otherwise there would have been a lot of pressure on us to make 'Love Me For a Reason' go straight in at No. 1.

Not another autograph!

Ronan pits his strength against a lemon

We now hate the song 'Working My Way Back To You'. We recorded 'Love Me For a Reason' last August. When it was released in Ireland in the autumn, it got to No. 1, and then it entered the UK charts at No. 10 and climbed to No. 2, behind East 17's 'Stay Another Day'. Again we weren't disappointed about it not going to No. 1 because it meant that we could release 'Key To My Life' without too much pressure.

'Key To My Life' was written by me, Mikey and Steve. It means different things to each of us, as we all wrote sections ourselves. I like it a lot as it's a big soppy song.

It's fun being on tour but it's lonely being away from home. On the *Smash Hits* Roadshow it was exciting to meet all the new fans, but it was a lot of work and we spent a lot of time travelling around on the coach. We slept most of the time. Optimystic and Shampoo were on our coach. Shampoo were total eejits, God love them. But Optimystic were lovely. We became friends of theirs, and we try to keep in touch with the three guys, Bryn, Stuart and Ian. We've also become friends with Deuce, while East 17 are also great mates.

The *Smash Hits* Roadshow was incredible. It broke us in the UK. *Smash Hits* were so good to us – they were brilliant. When we played in Dublin with the roadshow last November, it was great to come home as a lot of people in the UK hadn't heard us before. It showed the rest of the bands how big we are in Ireland. When they played 'Love Me For a Reason', at the finale, all the bands, including East 17, came out and sang it.

We found out the day before the *Smash Hits* Poll Winners' awards that we had won Best New Act on the roadshow. We were delighted. I met Robbie from Take That before the show in the Docklands Arena in London in early December. He was really friendly. He came over and congratulated us on our single.

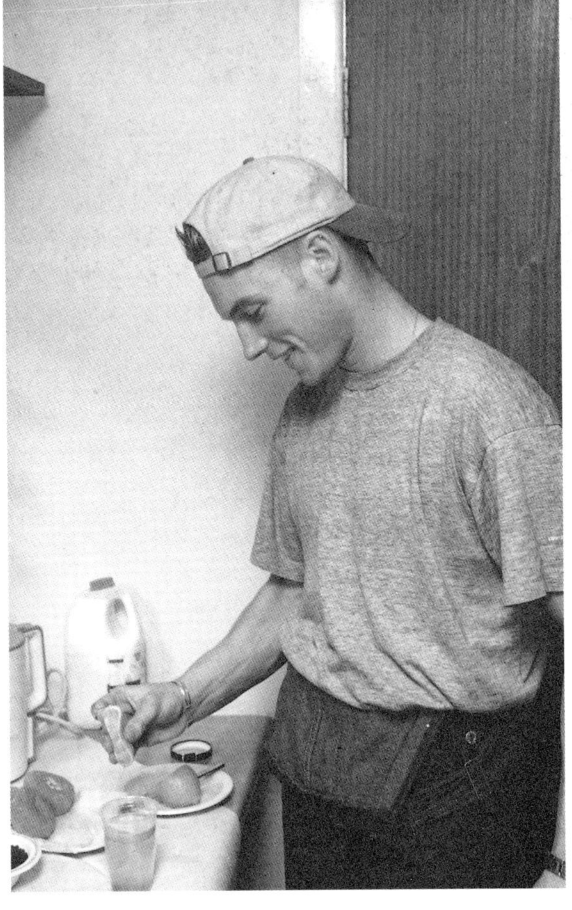

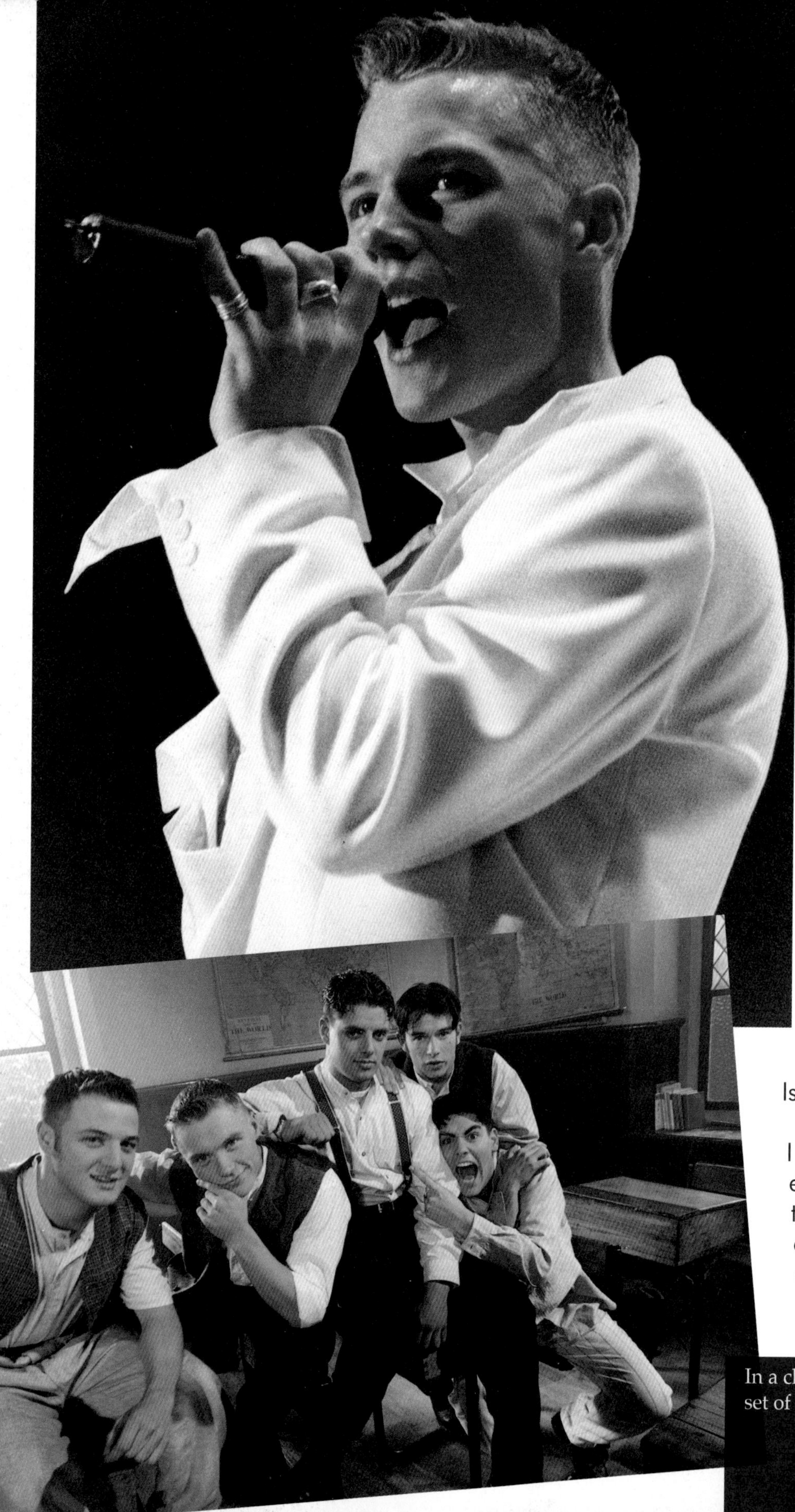

In a class of their own. On the set of the video shoot for 'Key To My Life'

We found out later that afternoon that we had entered the UK charts at No. 10 with 'Love Me For a Reason'. We were thrilled to have made the top ten. We went to the party afterwards and met loads of people. I had a good chat with Sean Maguire, whose Dad, like mine, is from Cavan. Then we came back to Ireland for the show at the Point in Dublin. We only had a week for rehearsals, and we were thrilled that so many fans went. We never thought we'd sell it out, and we were on such a high afterwards.

We finished off most of our debut album in London after Christmas and had a good time with our producer, Ray Hedges. We were living in an apartment in Victoria in London. It was mad: we were all cooking our own food, and we were lucky enough not to get food poisoning. We left the place in bits!

Like any family, we do have our moments in Boyzone when we have our fights, but we really are good mates. The lads think it's funny that I'm considered the most sensible member of the band. I've always been very responsible, probably because I had to grow up so fast after my brothers left home.

We're now flying all over Europe on promotional trips, and we find that fun. I liked Italy a lot. We're doing really well all over Europe, and we even got to No. 1 in Israel.

If Boyzone hadn't worked out, I always knew I could go into something else, such as acting or even a solo career. But things are going great – they couldn't be better. I wouldn't want to be doing anything else. I've always wanted to be something; I was always afraid of being a nobody.

STEVE
GATELY

Baby Steve with his Mum, Margaret

Two-year-old Steve poses in his *Muppet Show* t-shirt

Family

I was born in the Rotunda Hospital in Dublin on 17 March 1976, St Patrick's Day.

I have three brothers and one sister. The oldest, Mark, is 24 and married. Then there's Michelle, who's 23. Alan is 20 and Tony is 13. Tony is going to the same Christian Brothers school that I went to. Alan is an artist. Michelle is out in Sandyford in south Dublin, and she works in a hotel as a supervisor. She's also married, to Alan. Mark was out of work but he's back now after he got injured on a building site.

My Mam, Margaret, works in the local school and my Dad, Martin, used to do painting and decorating. I think my Mum is a great person, totally mad. She acts like my secretary, going through all the fan mail and answering the door to all the girls who come round. She looks and acts like Bette Midler!

My Granny is still alive, and she lives in Kilbarrack. She sometimes sleeps in my room when I'm away. I don't think she understands that I've become successful with a band. I think she's a bit blind. My sister went to see her one day wearing a scarf on her head, and Granny said, 'Your hair is looking lovely'. She's a gas character.

It was grand growing up around where I live in Seville Place, which is in the north inner city. It's not as bad as some people think it is. Once you were in the right circle of friends, you were all right. A lot of them are now in college.

The area where I live does have a bad drugs problem, and some of my friends who I grew up with are in a bad way, which is why I'm very much anti-drugs.

A friend of mine died from taking heroin, but no one seemed to know he was on drugs. I have never touched them and I never will. I even gave up drinking, except for shorts now and again.

My Haunted House!

I believe quite strongly in astrology. A psychic once told me my fortune out at RTE (Irish TV station). She told me I was psychic too. My Mam says the same thing, but I don't know if it's true.

I do sense things like ghosts. There's actually a ghost in my Mam's bedroom! She'll tell you that herself. When I was a kid we were living in Sheriff Street flats, and there was this ghost of a man who used to come out. I used to see him all the time, and I'd scream. I was around four when I saw him for the first time walking around the flat, and he used to come out every night.

Then we moved over here, to Seville Place, and I could see nothing. But about a year later the ghost must have followed us. When my Mam was going to bed she used to hear a strange voice.

One Easter, the Easter eggs, which were on top of the wardrobe, got thrown across the room by themselves. The hairdrier goes on by itself there too. My brother Alan came in one night to the bedroom and asked, 'Dad, have you got a light for my cigarette?', and the lighter just got thrown off the wardrobe. It's pretty cold in that room too; it's the coldest room in the house. I will not go into my Mam's bedroom now, although if it's daytime and I need the hairdrier I'll run in and out as fast as I can. I believe the ghost is a man who used to live in the flat before us. His name was Mr Jordan. We had the priest in to bless the house because of the ghost. I haven't seen the ghost in a long time. He's old, tall and skinny and wears a suit. My Mam says he was a really holy man who went to Mass every day and lived until he was over 90. She says he reared a lovely family and one of his sons became a doctor.

The psychic's daughter gave me a precious stone which brings out psychic powers and gives protection from evil spirits. I wear it all the time around my neck. I also tend to be able to make good judgments about people.

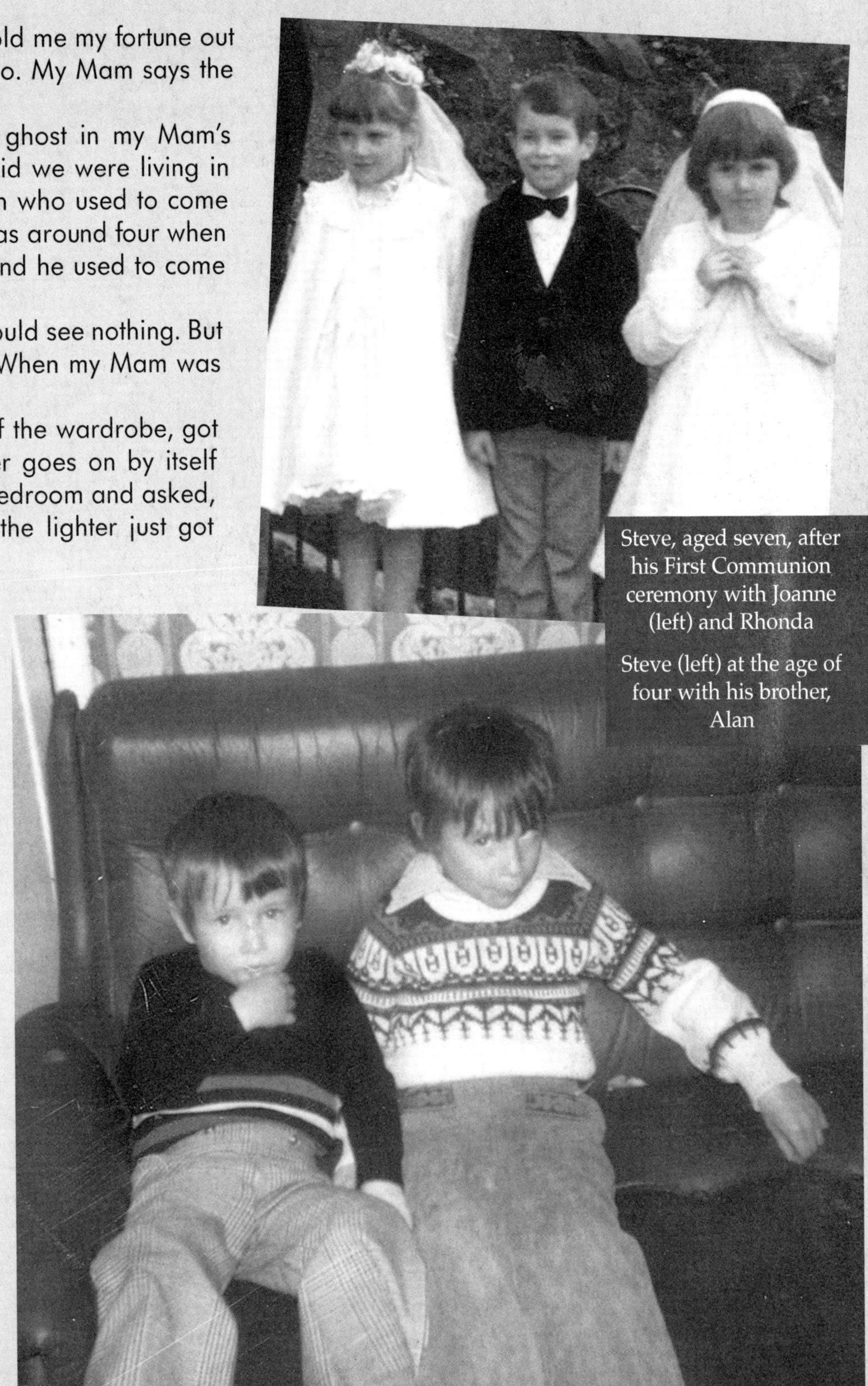

Steve, aged seven, after his First Communion ceremony with Joanne (left) and Rhonda

Steve (left) at the age of four with his brother, Alan

School

Pet dog Sting gets in the picture with Steve and his Mum, Margaret

Steve at his Confirmation with his brother, Tony, sister, Michelle, Mum, Margaret, and Dad, Martin

I went to the local primary school, St Laurence O'Toole's. I screamed the first day I went to school, when I was about four. My Mam and her mate brought me along. I went in and I started crying. My Mam's friend gave me some money, but I started shouting, 'I'm not going in, I'm not going in!' I started kicking her leg. But I had to go.

Miss Reynolds, my first teacher, was always really nice – she used to tell stories. She was sweet, and I'd like to see her again. When the classes changed each year, every class used to want to be taught by her. Then I had a teacher called Miss Combe. She wasn't nice at all. She had a really deep voice and was very strict. I also had the principal, Bean Ui Copeland. She was a really nice lady too. There was one teacher who wouldn't let me go to the toilet one day, so I sat there and went in my trousers. You had to ask in Irish if you wanted to go to the toilet. She was in the middle of something and wouldn't let me go. My Mam found out and gave out to her.

Joanne Barret was my best friend when I was young. I made my First Communion with her and Rhonda Byrne. I kind of classed Joanne as my cousin more than anything else. Her Mum, Maire, is my Mam's best friend. I call her my Aunty.

I loved English at primary school, particularly writing and poetry. We did musicals, and I always got a big role. I played the lead in *Joseph and the Amazing Technicolor Dreamcoat*. They made me wear this long coat. There was also one called *Old Ned*. It was an all boys' school, but for the plays they mixed the boys and girls.

After St Laurence's, I went to the Christian Brothers primary school when I reached first class. The teachers there were all right.

In primary school my best friend was Traner Mitchell. I hung around with him for years and years. I think he's working on a building site now, and I still keep in touch with him. My first teacher there was Mr Bailey, who I liked.

I then went to the North Strand Technical School, which was a bit of a change going on to second level. All my friends went to O'Connell schools, but my Mam wanted me to go to the North Strand. The first day I went into secondary school, I thought to myself, 'This is a whole new school, and I'm not going to be bullied.' But on that same day, I picked a fight with the biggest bloke in my class. His name was Stephen Gleeson, and I thought that if I could beat him I'd be left alone. Everyone then looked up to me, and no one touched me for the whole five years. I never bullied anyone – I just wasn't going to let anyone bully me. On that first day, he was ordering people around, and then he came over to me. He started it so I smacked him a few. We got on afterwards.

I loved Irish but when I went to the North Strand I couldn't get the hang of it. I liked most subjects there. I hated technical drawing, maybe because of the teacher. My best subjects would have been art, English and science. I loved drawing landscapes. There is an embankment with train tracks beside the school, and we used to draw that. I got five honours and two passes in the Junior Certificate.

I used to hate most sports in school but I liked gymnastics and I loved swimming. I used to go to Sean McDermot Street swimming-pool every Friday. I also did a lot of running competitions, 100-metre sprints in particular.

Declan Shine was my best mate throughout secondary school. We used to get into loads of mischief, like hiding things on the teacher or throwing books at the blackboard. We played pranks, mostly on our French teacher, Miss Ferero. When I first went to the school, there was a beautiful teacher who was only about 20. She was from France, and her name was something like Miss Shampoo! She was the first teacher I had a crush on.

After one term at the North Strand, when I was 16, I went to Marino College. There were two blokes, including me, in a class of 24 girls. I liked that class and made loads of friends. I met a girl called Nelly Conroy there, and we used to go out every Saturday night.

But I left Marino College after a few months and went back to the North Strand because I didn't get on with one of the teachers. When we went into her class, her mouth never stopped. I never did my homework for her – I was never really any good at it.

The North Strand took me back immediately. I got on really well with the principal, Mr Raleigh. I was there for a good while, about a year. I was studying for my Leaving Certificate, but my teachers knew what I wanted to do. They said that if I wanted something, I should get out and do it. When I left school, in about January 1994, Mr Raleigh said he'd take me back if it didn't work out. I left just before my Leaving Certificate. It was a choice I made, and I can always go back if I want to.

I was in O'Connell's Boys Club when I was around the age of 12. I used to do canoeing, sailing, swimming, mountaineering, all sorts of things. It was great. We used to go canoeing down the country, down by the lakes. I used to like the water, but then I'm a water sign, Pisces.

When I was young I was in a local dance troupe called Black Magic for about five years. There was about 12 of us, and I was one of four lads. We used to do dances in the local hall, and when I was 13 we won the All-Ireland disco-dancing competition in the Mansion House.

Steve rolls up his sleeves and gets down to work

Work

I was 14 when a friend, James Rafter, and I got our pictures taken by the International Modelling agency and did an interview. They called us back, we did a course and then we did some modelling of clothes for some department stores. We used to have to go up to Butlins every Wednesday to do a fashion show and dance routines. I then went to Assets modelling agency when I was about 16. I was interested in all forms of entertainment.

I got my first job when I was 16, when I did a bit of bar work in a local pub, Humphries, which is near the Five Lamps, where I live. I did shifts in the daytime, Saturdays and Sundays and some nights. I was paid about £4 an hour there, but I didn't like the work.

I also worked for a month during the holidays in the Olympia Theatre, cleaning glasses. I'd be there the whole night, cleaning glasses on my own. I loved it – I didn't feel lonely. I met the singer Mary Black there once and got talking to her. My first pay-packet was for £180, and I went out and got a really expensive pair of Adidas runners. I know the pay might seem a lot but I had to work until six o'clock in the morning. I had to lie about my age – I said I was 18 but I was 16.

When I left school I worked in Makullas clothes shop in Suffolk Street in Dublin. That was about two months after I joined the band, and I worked part time, for around three days a week. It was just for a couple of months and I was paid about £4 an hour. People started recognising me in the shop – I think there's still fan mail left there for me.

Film Star

My interest in drama started when I was at school on the North Strand. One teacher who used to help me was Miss Higgins, who used to do workshops with me. She told me I had talent and brought me out of myself a bit. I did loads of drama there. We did drama workshops, *Juno and the Paycock*. I also did drama outside the school. I went to a youth club, and we did a play there which was shown in the City Arts Centre. I later did an acting course at the Gaiety Theatre one summer a couple of years ago.

My first TV appearance was for *Jo Maxi* (an Irish youth show). I was 16 and I had directed a play called *Whether You Like it or Not*, performed by a group based in Coolock called Walk to Talk. I had been to see one of their plays and thought it was brilliant. I asked about joining and they accepted me. We did plays in the City Arts Centre and the Project Arts Theatre. Anyway, they chose me to direct this play. It basically involved telling this group of 12 people what to do. Most of them were a lot older than me. I was chancing my arm a bit.

I was also an extra on *In the Name of the Father*. I was on the roof throwing bricks. I met Daniel Day Lewis and he was a really nice guy, as was Liam Neeson, who came to visit the set. I'd love to take a leading role in a film, though I was glad that my part was cut from *In the Name of the Father*. But you can see me for a split second in *The Commitments*. There's a market scene at the very start, where me and my Mam are haggling for stuff. I was supposed to be selling wooden frames for pictures and my Mam was just looking at clothes. Because the film was shot around here, most people from the area took part in it.

I went for an audition for another film, *Oh, Mary, This London*, for Channel 4. I went for the main part but I wasn't what they were looking for. Then, just a few weeks ago, I was in the studio doing photographs when I heard Keith on the phone saying, 'No, he's not here.' So then I got on the phone and started talking to this girl, who it turned out had auditioned me. She told me that I was well into acting and that I stood out a mile. She said she was surprised the director didn't pick me. I also got into the final auditions at the Gaiety Theatre for a part in the *Snow Queen*, but I didn't get that either because I was too young.

HOW WE MET

I never took any singing lessons, but after the fashion shows at Butlins I used to do karaoke for the whole bunch who were with us. One night about four years ago there was a karaoke at the local North Star Hotel. I was drinking 7-Up then! Me and Michelle Whelan got up and sang 'Endless Love'. Michelle is a friend from a club I used to be in that looks after under-privileged children, where I used to teach drama. We won the karaoke and got £100, which we split. I think it all went that night! I always noticed that I could reach high notes. The first time I went to a concert was to see MC Hammer. I got a free ticket and went.

I remember hearing about the auditions for Boyzone and was desperate to have a go. I had no contact number and no details about the auditions, so I eventually rang up the *Star* newspaper in Dublin, and Eugene rang back with Louis Walsh's number. I was delighted, and went along to the Ormond Centre.

The auditions were nerve-wracking. I remember seeing all these blokes there and saying to myself, I haven't a chance in the world. After my turn, I was called back again, and the final audition, which took place over a week, was really tense. We all sang 'Careless Whisper' for the first two auditions. Then I sang Lionel Richie's 'Hello' and 'Right Here Waiting' by Richard Marx. I remember that Mikey gave me a lift home from the auditions that night.

At the end of the third audition, I was told that I was in the band, and I thought it was really cool. Then we went on the *Late Late Show* the next night and did a dance routine to 'Burn, Baby, Burn' by Clubhouse. All my friends were delighted. There was a major difference between our first appearance on the *Late Late Show* and our second, as we had only been together for a few hours when we went on the first time.

It's amazing just how far we have come.

We've been working so hard over the last year that we only got time off for a holiday last January. I went to Morocco, where I had an accident on a moped. I had been riding it for about three hours around the town when I skidded on a corner and scraped my right side and leg on the gravel. I had to go to hospital to get patched up.

If Boyzone hadn't worked out, I would have liked to have done something to become famous. I was always acting, so I would probably have tried that field.

We've been compared to Take That. When I saw them live in Dublin last year, they were really, really good. I had a good chat with Robbie at the *Smash Hits* Poll Winners' awards. He thought we were great and he's a really nice guy.

We're the first successful Irish pop group. There are some good rock bands in Ireland but we're the first real pop group, and we're proud of that.

In five years' time, I'd like to be offered big roles in films and I'd like to be still writing music. I want to have a house in Dalkey or Killiney in south Dublin beside the sea and a house somewhere else in the world where I can stay during the summer. It's lovely around Killiney and Dalkey. Bono and Chris de Burgh both live there. All I want is to be happy in life and have enough money to get by.

A merry Steve

KANGOL
KEITH
DUFFY

Family

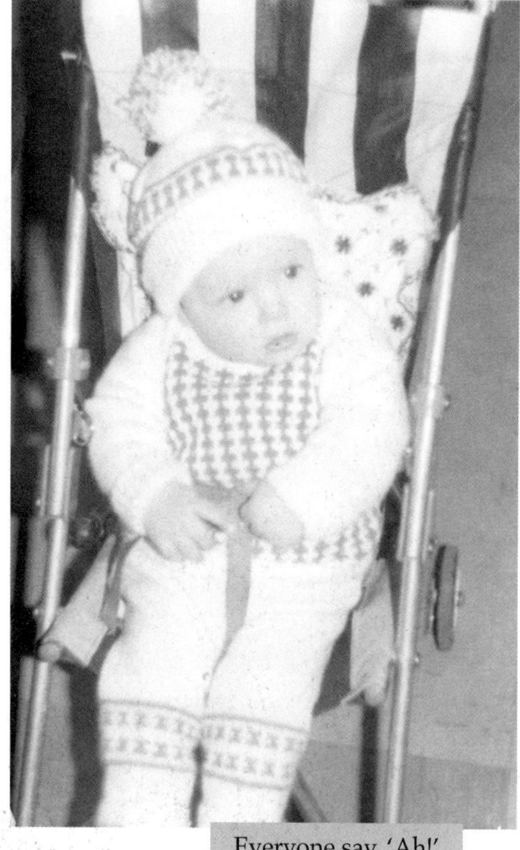

I was born in the Rotunda Hospital in Dublin on 1 October 1974. I have two brothers and I'm in the middle. John, my younger brother, is 15 and then there's Derek, who's 22.

Derek did four years in civil engineering and qualified with a degree. He couldn't get a job in Ireland so he went to work in London, but he recently came back home again. They gave him a six-month trial and said he could have a job and a company car, but he turned it down as he wanted to come home. He's going back to college for two years to do his masters. He also has his girlfriend over here, which was another reason why he came back. It was a big move for him, and it was the first time the family was broken up. It was very upsetting when he moved away.

John is still in secondary school, doing his Junior Certificate. He's the baby of the family, big time – he's spoiled rotten! A lot of girls go out with him because he's my brother. He doesn't give me any thanks!

My Mum, Pat, is a hairdresser. She also does a lot of voluntary work for the Alzheimer hospital, doing the patients' and nurses' hair. My Dad, Sean, works in Frawley's department store in Thomas Street in Dublin, where he's the manager. We have a pet dog, Socks, and a rabbit called Shoes. Get it?!

My best friend is Gavin Corcoran, who I've known since the age of six, and we played Gaelic football and hurling together for years. I spend a lot of time in Gavin's house, and I like talking to his Mum in her kitchen.

Everyone say, 'Ah!' Keith at six months

Two-year-old Keith with his brother, Derek

All aboard – Keith, aged two, on holiday in Tramore

School

I can barely remember my first day in primary school, an all boys' school called Belgrove in Clontarf. I remember my father bringing me right into the school, right into the classroom, and settling me down. I just remember when he left me, I started bawling my eyes out and I ran after him and grabbed on to his leg. I wouldn't let go, even though he was going off to work. One of the teachers had to take me off him.

That was Miss Hagan, my first teacher. She was a lovely girl – she must have been about 24. I had her for two years, while I was doing the basics.

Then in first class I had a little old lady called Miss Brosnan. In second class I had a girl called Miss Cummins, who was very strict. In third class I had a teacher called Miss Moran. She was sound, a really good teacher, and we had great crack with her. Then for fourth, fifth and sixth class I had her brother, Mr Moran. He was also great crack. He was the hurling teacher in the school, and I played Gaelic football and hurling from the age of seven until I was 18.

In primary school I got bullied but I also bullied too. When my older brother was in the school and I got bullied, he'd get the guys back. As I grew up in school, I became a bit of a bully myself. We didn't do anything bad though – we didn't hurt anybody or bash anybody up. There was a gang of us from my class who were the heads of the school. We used to walk around the schoolyard, and nobody would get in our way. They'd all scatter fast.

My friends in school then were Barry Shields, Keith Flanagan, Stuart Kelly, Darren Wallace and Christian Kinsella. They still are very tough guys. We were the athletic guys in the school, and if there were any competitions – Gaelic football, hurling, running, anything – we would win them. We beat every class in the school.

The first time I was suspended was in primary school. I was in sixth class and the priest was in lecturing us about our Confirmation, coming up to Hallowe'en. I let off three stink-bombs, and the stink in the classroom was unbelievable. They found out it was me.

I was in Norma Barry's School of Dancing for years. Her sister, Billie Barry, also runs a prominent school of dancing. I joined them when I was five and stayed until I was 12. We did a lot of pantomimes and plays, such as *Lullaby of Broadway, 42nd Street*, all that type of thing.

In sixth class in primary school we did a play which we made up ourselves, and I had the lead part, a punk rocker. It was based on the kids in the school. We made up our own songs and our own dance routines too – it was a bit like *West Side Story*.

When I went to secondary school it was a big change. It was the worst three years of my life. I went to Ard Scoil Ris on Griffith Avenue, and everybody there had already been to the same primary school together. I was an outsider to them. They were all from Marino – I was from Donaghmede. I went there because that's where my older brother, Derek, went to school. I had to go into that school and make a name for myself. The others all lived in the same area, and because I was from Donaghmede they thought I was a scumbag. They thought I was a bit of a hoodie, as it was called at the time.

I didn't get on very well

A trendy Keith, aged 12, on his Confirmation day

Even at the age of 12, Keith (front middle) had a starring role in his primary school musical

there. I got picked on an awful lot. There was a disco called the Oasis on every Saturday night down in the school, and there were girls' schools called the Dominican College and Maryfield up the road. So Ard Scoil Ris, the community college and Maryfield used to go to this disco. To be quite honest, I had a lot of girls into me for some reason. I never had any problems scoring in the disco, and it turned out there were an awful lot of fellows in the school who were jealous of me. There were certain girls who they fancied, and these girls were coming over to me. So they gave me a bit of a rough time over it.

Keith, aged 10, with his brother John and his first bike

I was in plenty of fights. For my first three years at Ard Scoil Ris I was in quite a lot. The worst one was when I was in third year and came out with a black eye. It was one time when three or four boys started on me in the football field beside our school and I got a few slaps. But the next day I got a few of the lads from where I lived to come down, and we kicked lumps out of them. I never got any hassle again.

I never got really close to any of the teachers there. Mr Daly, the maths teacher, was a friend of my Ma's so I kind of got on all right with him. But the teachers in the school didn't like me, maybe because I was from a different area.

My best friends in the world now are the guys I went to school with after I left Ard Scoil Ris. I went to a place called Plunket School on the Swords Road. I did my Leaving Certificate there, and the guys there were the best friends I ever had. Also, they hadn't all been to the same school before, which helped.

I was a bit of a messer in that school and got into a lot of trouble. My favourite subjects there were technical drawing and construction studies, which involved woodwork at that time. I had a great time for those two years, doing all the subjects I wanted to, including engineering. I got a good Leaving Certificate.

I then went to third level and did architectural drawing in a pre-college course at Colaiste Ide in Finglas. I got a London City and Guilds award for computer design. I did just a year there. Although it was a two-year course, when I went back for the second year I left to join the band.

At Plunket School I was suspended three times, just for general messing: not turning up for classes, smoking in the classroom, not turning up for school on Wednesday morning when there were Irish classes on.

I was once nearly expelled from Plunket's when the whole class was suspended. We all used to meet down at the school gate at nine o'clock in the morning and go into the city centre, rather than go to our classes. We used to go to the arcades and play a bit of pool. One day we went on the bonk and met four of the other lads from the class, and we were seen meeting them getting on the bus.

When we came back we went into a little shop up the road, and our English teacher, Mr Kenny, came in and caught us. We were all pretty gargled, having had three or four beers in town. He dragged us back down to the school. We couldn't care less, as we were having a great laugh and we were drunk. We were hauled up to our foremaster, Mr Fox, and he sent letters back to our parents telling them to come in. When they did we were told we were being expelled. My Dad got me off, and I did my Leaving Certificate there.

I drank in the fields near my home when I was 16. I was hanging around with Christian Kinsella, who I had known since we were very young, and also Mark Flanagan and Gavin Corcoran. Christian is now an apprentice printer in Finglas, but I haven't seen him since I joined the band.

Sport

I loved Gaelic football and hurling ever since I started primary school, and I continued playing both games until I was 18. I was captain for most of my school teams. I also played soccer, at under-nine and under-11, for Donaghmede boys.

I preferred playing midfield in Gaelic football, and I played right-half-forward in hurling. I played for the club side Trinity Gaels and also for my schools. We won the Dublin North-East Championship, the Dublin schools and colleges tournament, when I was at Ard Scoil Ris. I also played for the Dublin under-16 team and the minor team. I represented Dublin for three years. We were beaten by Wexford in the Under-16 All-Ireland hurling final.

With the Dublin minor football team, I only played a few matches, but I played in Croke Park a few times. I got trials for Stella Maris soccer club, and then I went back to the Gaelic football.

I would have loved to continue playing Gaelic football and hurling but I used to work with my Dad in Frawley's on Saturdays, which meant that I had to miss training for the Dublin under-21s, so I never made the team.

I once got a bad head injury, a crack to the skull, when I was playing hurling and ended up in hospital for three weeks. When I came out I had to work with my Dad on Saturdays, so I didn't get a chance to play. I haven't played in a long time, but I'd like to again.

Ace hurler Keith, aged 14, after winning the Dublin Championships with Ard Scoil Ris. He's third from the left in the middle row

Work

My first job was at a place called Clare Manor, which was a golf driving-range. I was 14, and we used to have to pick up all the balls. We used to get paid £2.50 an hour. I saved up and bought myself a mountain-bike. It was great because I hadn't got a penny then and I was looking for a job at the time.

Pat's drumming is too much for Keith

My next job was at the Fingal House in Clontarf, where I worked as a lounge boy and hotel receptionist. Then I joined my Dad at Frawley's in Thomas Street, working part time for four years. I was a sales assistant in the hardware department, and I got paid about £3.50 an hour – a very well-paid job. I also sometimes worked part time for a company doing security at big concerts. I was then with Makullas clothes shop for a while when the band was set up, just to give me a bit of pocket money.

HOW WE MET

I've played the drums all my life, and I started playing with the Donaghmede All Stars marching band when I was about eight. I went to classes in Donaghmede school. The band is now called the Dublin All Stars.

When I was about 16, I got a tax rebate from a part-time job for about £500 or £600. I had never had that much money in my life. I borrowed another £100 and I bought a kit of drums. They are now in my bedroom at home, but I started learning to play them in a shed at the bottom of my garden as it was a bit noisy.

Then I met a session player, Kevin Brady, who gave me a few tips. I joined a covers band called Toledo Moon. I knew the drummer, Stuart Kierans, and I filled in for him once or twice. They were a fantastic band – they didn't need me. I thought they would make it. They used to play all over Dublin.

When I was 18 I joined a Gothic band called This Burning Effigy. I had had longish hair ever since I went to secondary school, but around the time I was in the band I had hair down to my shoulders. All I remember is going for an audition and bashing some drums with them. They were pretty impressed. I just jammed with them for a while.

It was a coincidence that I got into Boyzone. I had seen all the pictures of Shane appearing in the newspapers and read stories that he was going to be involved in an Irish answer to Take That. Shane and I have known each other since we were young. We didn't hang around together, but we knew each other by sight. We were two good-looking blokes around the area. I then started going out with Shane's sister, Alison, who was the same age as me. Her house was around the block from mine, so I used to go to the pictures with her and sometimes Shane would come along too.

Anyway, I heard about the auditions for this new band. I knew that Shane and this other guy, Mark, were trying to form a band, so one day I asked them to get me an interview with Louis Walsh. I told them to tell him I was interested in joining the band but nothing came of it.

Three weeks went by and I never heard a word. By pure coincidence, I was dancing on the stage at the Pod nightclub in Dublin one night when Louis came up and asked me whether I was interested in joining a pop group. I asked him if we were going to make lots of money, and he said, 'Yeah!' I told him that I knew Shane and Mark and that I had been looking for him for the last three weeks. So I went up and did the audition.

I didn't go for the first one, but I went for the second and sang Billy Joel's 'Piano Man'. I wasn't that sure I'd get into the band, as there was an awful lot of talented people there. I also had to do a dance to Right Said Fred's 'I'm Too Sexy'. I was the same as anyone else there, hoping that I would get into the band. It was very nerve-wracking. I remember being in the corridor with all the guys going for the audition, and then going into the studio and not knowing anyone in there. Six of us were picked, then two dropped out and we got Mikey in.

I had no idea the band would get so big, because it was so slow when it started off. We even had to do part time jobs to keep going at the start. The first single, 'Working My Way Back To You', did very well when it came out in Ireland. Then 'Love Me For a Reason' took off in the UK after getting to No. 1 here. The reaction from the fans on the *Smash Hits* Roadshow was unbelievable. They were so nice to us, even though they didn't know us.

A lark in the park

There are five of us in the band because it looks good on stage: three at the back, two at the front. That's all. We've been called the Irish Take That, but that's stupid. If there were four of us, we'd have been the Irish Bad Boys Inc.; with three we'd be the Irish EYC. It's ridiculous. When we won the *Smash Hits* Poll Winners' award for best new act on the roadshow it was a massive two fingers to all the begrudgers who said we'd never make it and who were being cynical. My mates and family were delighted, and that's what matters.

But I'm still the same bloke now, I've still got my feet on the ground. I'm not a big-headed bloke. I had a hard life before I got it, but this work isn't that easy either. I'd still like to live in Dublin, but I'd like to be as near as possible to the country, somewhere like Kinsealy or Malahide, which would be close to my home in Donaghmede.

I don't think success will change any of us. We've great crack together. I've now got four mates who'll stand by me through thick and thin, and I've Louis Walsh to thank for that.

Boyzone after the Phoenix Park concert

MIKEY GRAHAM

Family

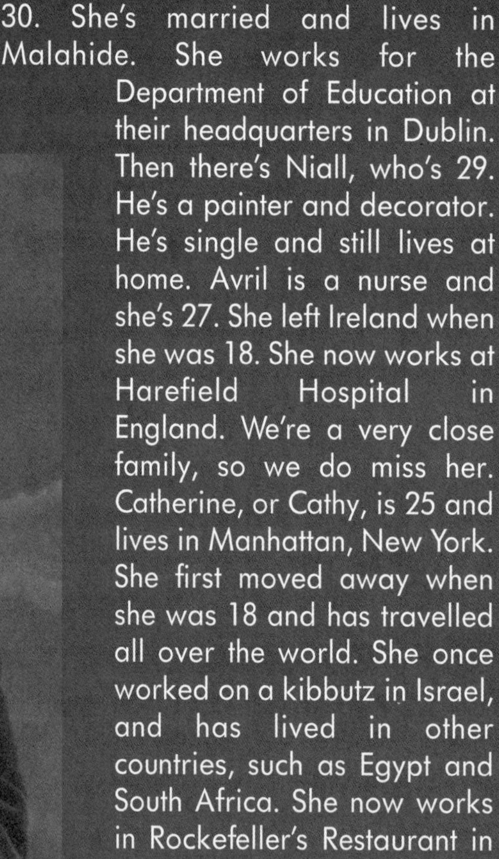

An angelic Mikey makes his First Communion at the age of six

I was born in the Rotunda Hospital, Dublin, on 15 August 1972. I have just one brother but I have five sisters. The oldest in my family is Yvonne, who's 30. She's married and lives in Malahide. She works for the Department of Education at their headquarters in Dublin. Then there's Niall, who's 29. He's a painter and decorator. He's single and still lives at home. Avril is a nurse and she's 27. She left Ireland when she was 18. She now works at Harefield Hospital in England. We're a very close family, so we do miss her. Catherine, or Cathy, is 25 and lives in Manhattan, New York. She first moved away when she was 18 and has travelled all over the world. She once worked on a kibbutz in Israel, and has lived in other countries, such as Egypt and South Africa. She now works in Rockefeller's Restaurant in New York. Then there's the twins, Claire and Debbie. They're both 24. Claire is married and lives up the road. She works in an office in Dunne's Stores, while Debbie still lives at home and works in catering.

My Mum, Sheila, is a housewife. We're very close and sometimes have long chats with each other in the kitchen in the mornings or in the evening. We send cards to each other addressed to 'My pal'. My father, William, or Billy as he's known, is a carpenter. At one stage I thought about becoming a carpenter. I once had the opportunity to take it up but my interest lay in mechanics.

I didn't mind growing up as the baby in my family – it was a bit like the Brady Bunch. I didn't get too much special treatment. Because Niall was a lot older than me, I didn't have that close a bond with him. When I was quite young, he was in his teenage years and he went away a lot.

I've always lived in Kilmore West in Coolock. It was okay growing up there – no different from anywhere else. There were some tough kids and some who were not so tough.

I remember my first pushbike, a chopper. I was about eight. What happened was that Niall had won one a few years earlier in a competition on Christmas Eve. Niall didn't really use it much, but when I reached the age where I could ride a bike I pestered my folks for one. It was a case of either getting a new bike or getting the other one stripped down, so we took it apart and did it up. I've been messing about with pushbikes since I was a kid. I'd even take radios and little motors apart. I loved making something out of them.

A lot of kids in the neighbourhood had bikes. I must have known 30 or 40 kids. We got up to the usual, like playing football and games, such as hide and seek.

School

I can remember my first day in low babies at Ardlea Primary School on the Ardlea Road. I was kicking and screaming and didn't want to go. I was four years of age, and my Mam had to tie me down and bring me in the pram. The principal of the school took me round all the classrooms but I didn't want to stay. She left me in one and I screamed the place down. My first teacher was someone who I didn't like at all. I used to tell my family that I liked her arms and her legs, but I didn't understand what her body was. She always used to grab me by the ears when I was naughty in the class. I had her for three years.

I went to school with a lot of the lads who lived in my area. My best friend then is still my best friend now, Shane Murray. He lives just five doors from me. He has a lot of brothers, and we were all friends. He has just come back from Manhattan, but he always knew that I was likely to join something like Boyzone.

At school I used to love religion, English and art. When I reached second class in primary school I went to St David's CBS on the Kilmore Road, and then I went to the secondary school part of St David's on the Malahide Road. Second class in primary was a big change, as my previous school was mixed. In second class I was taught by Mr McDonald, in third and fourth by Mr Keegan, while in fifth and sixth class I had Mr O'Brien. I liked Mr McDonald a lot and Mr Keegan was okay, but I didn't like Mr O'Brien.

One day, when I was in fifth class, me and three other lads were playing a game out in the yard and continued it in the toilet. I was hanging from the toilet wall, when I crashed into the sink and the whole lot came out of the wall. There was water everywhere. Everyone just scarpered, and we were lucky not to be caught.

Because we were in a gang, I didn't get into fights. There were groups of lads here and there, and there was general respect for each group. There was an odd fight here and there.

When I went to secondary school, St David's, I was scared stiff. I heard that the older boys there used to throw you down the big iron staircase when you went into first year, but it never happened to me. I got on very well with the teachers. I think I made them laugh – I was a real joker. My friend, Luke, went to another school but Willy and Stephen went to St David's, although they weren't in my class. There was another fellow,

Confirmation boy Mikey at the age of 12

'Are you looking at me?' asks Mikey

school since the age of five, and I kept going until I was 15. I went there because my sisters were in it. On my first day there, too, I was crying. It was mostly dancing and singing, and we did some pantomimes. I also did some TV advertisements. One was for Mikado biscuits, which involved a whole lot of us running around the factory, supposedly making the biscuits. I was about ten at the time. The biggest one I did was for the ESB (Irish electricity board). I was a schoolboy who left a warm house and then came back in the evening out of the rain. That would also have been when I was about ten. I was a superstar in my area because of it!

There were very few boys in the Billie Barry school. Shane and I were there together, and Billie took a particular shine to us. I think it was because we were real boys at heart. We were bold brats but we were good too. We weren't her usual sissy-type fellows. There were a lot of lads there who were lickarses.

Gordon Quinn, who was in all my classes right through to third year, and then we split. He's one of my best friends. Another three of the lads on my road were in my class in secondary school so there was a gang of us again, which meant we were okay. Shane's older brother, Garret, was in my class, so I had someone else on my side.

I was always good at English and I liked woodwork and technical drawing. I liked everything but I hated maths and I hated Irish. My first exam was the Group Certificate. There was a lot of pressure – everyone thought that if you didn't pass this, it was the end of the world – but I passed.

In first year we did *Joseph and the Amazing Technicolor Dreamcoat*, and I played the Pharaoh. I was sitting with my back to the audience when the chair was flung around and I had to sing, in an Elvis voice, a song with lines like 'I was rockin' by the river'. I was making a total idiot out of myself.

There was a music teacher at school but I didn't do the subject. I had been going to the Billie Barry

I did the *Late Late Show* toy show three times. The first time when I was about eight, it was nerve-wracking. Me and Shane had to dress up in red jackets and play the part of toy soldiers guarding a palace. In another show, we did an old-fashioned scene, in which we dressed up in grey suits and bowler hats. The next show had a 1950s' rock 'n' roll theme: the girls wore 1950s' dresses, and we wore crepe-soled shoes, drainpipe trousers and leather jackets. I left the show when I was about 15 – I think I had done everything I could do in it. I had done all my pantomimes, plays and TV shows. I couldn't really go any further.

I was also in the scouts, the 51st Kilmore, and the cubs from the age of seven. We went on annual camps, mostly in the Dublin and Wicklow mountains. I was good at knots, map-reading and first-aid. I was also in the Artane Boys Band when I was about 11. I used to play the drums, and I was in the band for two years. I started kick-boxing when I was 13 and continued until I was 19. I used to do it in Coolock Village, but I never threw my weight around, although I could look after myself.

Boyzone with Jack Charlton

·y being used as a pool cue

Work

When I left school, at 17, I went for an interview for a job as a mechanic in Ballsbridge and worked there for a year. The owner had promised me an apprenticeship if I served there for a year but it didn't happen so I had to leave to try to get it somewhere else. I went to work for a sign company, and then I worked on cabs. After that, I got a place at Annesley Motors in Ballybough.

I got my first car, a Fiat 127, when I was 17. It was a thrill to get it, and as I had an interest in mechanics I could start playing around with it. I got my very first wage-packet when I was about 14 and working part time as a shop assistant at Superquinn in Northside Shopping Centre. I wasn't the saving type, and I blew all the money. I also worked part time for a while as a porter in Clery's department store. Even when I was smaller, I used to do my own bob-a-jobs during the summer for the neighbours and made quite a lot of money for a young lad.

Mikey hits a high note

Boyzone trying to keep their feet on the ground

HOW WE MET

The first time I showed any interest in a band was with neighbours and friends when I was about seven. We went to Mark Kenny's shed and used tennis rackets as guitars and pots as drums.

I've been in a few bands. The last one I was in was called Ivory. Those guys were really brilliant musicians. I was the lead singer. We did a lot of cover stuff, such as Gary Moore and Eric Clapton. I joined after applying to an advertisement in *Hot Press* magazine, and we used to play around a few pubs.

I've always loved songwriting. I've written something like 70 songs now, and I'd like to be remembered for some pop classics, although I'm more of a rock fan than a fan of pop.

I remember hearing about the auditions for Boyzone on the radio when I was at work. I didn't think much about it until I got home and saw it in the newspaper.

My Dad and then my friends encouraged me to go. I went along, and I had to sing George Michael's 'Careless Whisper'. When I was called back again, I did Eric Clapton's 'Layla'. Then, the third time, I did Meatloaf's 'Two Out of Three Ain't Bad'. I wasn't disappointed when I was turned down initially for the band, as I knew there'd be something else for me. I had a strong feeling within me that it didn't matter, it would be okay. I was fairly happy when I was called back after one of the original members left. I went in, had a look at what was going on and decided to give it a go.

A lot of people who slag us off are just jealous. They see us on stage with thousands of screaming girls and think we've got it easy, but they don't see all the hard work behind the scenes. Many bands would not be able to cope with our workload. A lot of fellows would secretly love to be in our position. I had a feeling it would get big. I remember at the *Smash Hits* Roadshow that Ronan was saying he'd be happy if 'Love Me For a Reason' would chart in the UK top 20, and I told him, 'It's going all the way. It's going right to the top.' I predicted it, and I was delighted when it got to No. 2.

Mikey with his youngest fan

Reebok

GIRLS WILL BE GIRLS, FANS WILL BE FANS

Shane

I first started to take an interest in girls when I was about 14 or 15. I'm talking about girls from around where I live. I never went out with a girl from school. The girls I like are small, but not too small, with dark hair.

I kissed a girl for the first time when I was 12. It happened at Alison's party when there were about 20 girls sleeping over at our house. We played a game of dares, and someone dared me to kiss this girl. It was the worst mistake of my life. I remember it tasted horrible. It lasted three seconds, and I didn't kiss for a year after that.

I knew I was good looking but I never plucked up the courage to ask a girl out. It wasn't because I was big-headed and wanted them to come to me. It was just that I wasn't that kind of bloke. I also never had the confidence to ask anyone out, although when one girl asked me I went out with her for a while. Her name was Sinead. I think it happened when Derek got a car and we used to drive about. We just met that way.

I started going to night-clubs when I was 14, but I only went there to dance. I didn't really go to meet girls. The first time I was turned down by a girl was when I was about 14. I asked this girl to dance but she said no. I thought to myself, 'Well, I was only feeling sorry for her', and went away with my tail between my legs.

The first time I chucked a girl was when I was 16. I had been with her for about two months over Christmas but I didn't really love her. I told her it wasn't working out, so we split up.

The first love of my life was a girl called Gillian Lamb. She was 21, I was 17. I had my first real date with her, and we went to a club where it was hard to get a conversation going. I was really nervous, but it turned out all right.

I'd like to get married by the age of 22 and have four kids. I could never see myself getting involved with a fan, though. Getting involved with a fan is just the wrong thing to do. A fan is just after me or one of the other lads because we're famous. Fans don't understand what we're really like.

The fans are all nice girls, though. There are always some of them hanging around outside my house. They give me presents – things like chains and bracelets – especially at autograph sessions. Most seem to have my address now.

I've stopped going to places like Grafton Street in Dublin, especially on Saturdays, as a lot of fans seem to recognise me. It's pure madness trying to get rid of some fans. They just won't let go.

Ronan

At school there were never really any girls in my life, just my Mam and my sister. I remember my first kiss – I don't remember her name, but I remember the kiss. I was 13. We were at a party in Bayside. I didn't know how to kiss but she did! She was two or three years older than me and I never saw her afterwards so I can't have impressed her that much!

I like girls who have blonde hair, blue eyes and are about my own height.

Georgina was my first love but I don't get to see her much any more. I don't know if she loves me. Perhaps she feels left out because of my success. She's from Glasnevin and she's one of my best friends.

My first crush was in primary school, but I forget the girl's name. The problem was that she didn't like me, and when I asked her out she said no, so we never went out together. The first time I dropped a girl was also in primary school. I think I did it just to be cool, and neither of us were that bothered.

I had my first date at the age of 16. Again, I can't remember her name, but we went to see *Cry Freedom*. As I'm quite shy, I can never really talk to girls. All I can remember saying to her was, 'Are you okay?'

I'd like to get married, maybe when I'm 25 or 26, and have two or three children. I wouldn't like to be too young but I wouldn't like to be too old either. It's not wise now to have a relationship, but eventually I would like one. I am still a virgin but there's no reason for that.

I don't think I'm good looking – in fact, I think my nose is disgusting! I've been called Tin-Tin because of my hair ever since I went to school. I used to be a big Bros fan, and I styled it just like them. I used to be a fan of theirs – I even had some of their posters on my wall when I was younger!

I get recognised in a lot of places around town now. If I'm in Dublin city centre with another member of the band, like Steve, we get totally mobbed.

My family don't mind too much about fans calling to the house. I usually have a chat with them, and I have got to know quite a few regular faces. My Mam sometimes leaves the phone off the hook, as she gets pestered by a lot of fans ringing up for me.

Every time we go to the airport there are fans waiting to say goodbye or hello. It's getting crazy in the UK now too. Once, when we were on the way to *Top of the Pops*, a group of fans crashed into the back of our van. They carry mobile phones and let each other know where we are. When we stopped, we found five girls in the car aged about 16 or 17. Fortunately, they were okay. There have also been one or two moments when I have been concerned about fans fainting and being pulled over crash-barriers. I know there's good security but I worry that something might happen.

Hearing the screams when we go on stage gives me an incredible feeling. The adrenaline rush is amazing. Some of the girls are really forward. I spend half my life blushing. I do get aggravated now and again, as I have very little privacy and my social life is always being interrupted, but I wouldn't change it for the world.

Steve

Joanne Barret and I were best friends from an early age, and we made our First Communion together. We might have been friends, but she was the first girl I kissed. I was 12. That was early days, years ago. We were best buddies. She lived just underneath me in the flats, and we did loads together. We were great friends. She sends me birthday and Christmas cards every year, and I send them to her too. Joanne now has a kid and is pregnant again. They're not mine, though!

I like girls that have hair that curls naturally. I prefer them to have brown hair, a slim figure and be about five feet seven inches, my height. I was turned down by a girl for the first time at a disco. I asked her to dance, but she said no. She was really full of herself. I think she regrets not taking up my offer now!

I went out with about two girls in my class in Marino – Nelly Conroy and then a girl called Sandra. We just went to the pictures on dates, then the three of us remained really close friends. We didn't really have break-ups, just said to each other, 'This isn't working out too well'. I went out with Nelly for about a month and Sandra for three weeks.

I never went to a deb's ball, although I would have loved to. I nearly went to Nelly's deb's ball. The longest I've been out with a girl is nine months, with a girl from Glasnevin called Sharon about two or three years ago. I haven't seen her since, but I'd like to meet her again.

There was a girl I went out with for a while who had long, brown, curly hair, really dark skin and brown eyes. Her name was Anita McAuley. I went out with her until early last year. I took her to see M People in Dublin's National Stadium. That was our last date.

I bought loads of things for the girls: flowers, chocolates, jeans, tops. I used to go on day trips with some of the girls. I went to Holyhead for a day with Anita on the boat. We used to go to Bray and Dalkey.

I would like to get married one day and I'd like to have two kids, a boy and a girl. I haven't picked out my future wife yet!

I like Louise from Eternal. I also like Kelly from Deuce – we're really good friends but we never dated. There's a good few girls out there who make me say to myself, 'She's really cool'. I have to see how this Girlzone that they're trying to form in Dublin works out!

I now can't go anywhere without being recognised. Last year I was out looking for a birthday present when some fans stopped me on the street and offered to help. I eventually got a box of chocolates for my Mum, on their advice! Once some fans stopped me and asked what aftershave I liked. When I got home later, I found they had sent it to my house. I don't know how they got there before me.

My Mum has to act as a bit of a secretary, dealing with all the letters coming to the house. The only time I get peace and quiet is when I go to my sister's place.

Keith

I went out with a girl for the first time when I was in fifth class in primary school. Her name was Yvonne Keogh, and she was the first girl I ever kissed. We were babysitting at a friend's house and ended up kissing. I was afraid of my life that my Dad would find out, so I threw cold water on my lips. I went out with Yvonne for about three or four months. I was only 11. I used to go up to her house a lot but I had to make sure I was home by eight o'clock in the evening. I had my eye on Yvonne's best mate and went out with her afterwards but soon told her that it wasn't working out.

I went on my first real date when I was 12 or 13. We went to the pictures to see a matinee of *Pete's Dragon* but I can't remember the girl's name.

I used to be in Raheny Youth Club, in an old church in Raheny village. There was always music blaring there, and we'd play video games and table-tennis. If you fancied a girl in the club, at the end of the night you'd tell one of the lads, 'Fix me up with her, tell her I want to kiss her at the end of the night.' Then we'd go around to the back of the church and get off with these girls, and we would wait for the next Wednesday night to get off with another girl. I was only 14 or 15.

A lot of people in my area used to call me a poser or big-head. I didn't really fancy any of the girls in my area, and because I didn't go out with any of them they used to call me a poser. A lot of the fights I had at Ard Scoil Ris were with fellows who were jealous of me being fancied by the girls at the Oasis school disco.

Shane's sister was the first girl from the area I went out with. Shane was called a poser too. They were just jealous. I used to go out with an awful lot of girls from Clontarf, Marino, all over the place. I wasn't into going out with girls for a long time. A different girl every weekend would do me grand!

I went out with Shane's sister, Alison, when I was at Ard Scoil Ris. I met her on the bus when I was going to school around the time I was doing my Inter Certificate, when I was about 15. She asked me out, and we were together for about three or four weeks. I like girls that are smaller than me, and have black hair down to their shoulders or blonde hair. I love girls with green eyes.

I was turned down for the first time when I was 16 by a 21-year-old girl. I went to her deb's ball, and we had a great night. I rang

her a few times afterwards, asking what she was up to, but she completely blanked me. I think she was just shy.

The best snog I've ever had was with a girl I used to see a while ago called Lisa Smith. She gave my a lucky ring, which is my most prized possession.

I used to hang around with a gang of ten people when I was a regular at the Pod nightclub. Seven of them were gay, but it didn't bother me. I once met this model at the Pod who asked me to go home with her to Killiney. I agreed, and at about six o'clock in the morning we took off most of our clothes and went for a dawn swim.

I used to go weight-training five nights a week, as well as try to get to a gym in Moore Street on Saturday nights. I used to train at Universal Health in Kilmainham. I was in great shape for a while. I used to go to the Pod wearing just a vest, and the women would be all over me, saying I had a great body.

Then I was in the car smash with Shane. It happened in Easter 1994. We were speeding along when he went through a corner, and the car somersaulted five times. We were lucky to get out alive. I got an injury to my lower back and shoulders so I can't weight-train any more.

I've never had any problems getting a woman. There's an awful lot of blokes who can't get girls because they're so big-headed and the girls don't like them. I get on very well with girls.

I haven't had any really serious relationships. When I was about 18, I went out with a girl for about two months, but I did the bunk on her twice so I wasn't really serious about her. I blew her out but I can't tell you her name because she's going out with one of my mates. She's asked me back a couple of times but there was too much friction. I'm still good friends with her.

I don't want to get married until I'm at least 25. I'm too young for a really serious relationship – there's too much fun to be had. If I did get married to somebody, I'd love her to bits – I'd never do the dirt on her. I wouldn't be in favour of divorce because if you're getting married you make the commitment for ever. I'd vote against divorce ever coming to Ireland.

Some of our fans are gorgeous, and there is a temptation to sleep with them as you're bored and on the road. But I've always resisted! I don't, as a rule, mess around with any of the fans. But the day we forget about our fans will be the start of the end.

All we want to do is have as much fun as possible and make enough money to live off for the rest of our lives. I find the fans great, and I put up with pestering from a lot of them.

When my parents went on holiday last year, some fans even came and cooked for me each day and cleaned the house! The girls hoovered up and washed the dishes, and when Ronan and Steve called over one evening they cooked us all a meal.

It only takes two girls to stop you on Grafton Street to start a whole bunch of them mobbing you. That can cause problems. On Valentine's Day we got millions of cards, but my mother opened them as I was out of the country. She replies to a lot of the fans and sends autographs and writes back.

Mikey

I can remember my first kiss. I was eight, she was ten. She was a cousin of my neighbour, from England. I liked her, she liked me. I haven't a clue how it happened, but as she was leaving she gave me a kiss goodbye and slipped her tongue into my mouth. I didn't like it.

I had loads of friends who were girls at the Billie Barry School of Dancing but I never went out with any of them. I had a big crush on one of them when I was very young. I've seen her lately but I don't feel anything for her now.

I went to a lot of discos, and I loved the girls there. My first love was a girl called Sharon. We were both teenagers. I still love her in a way. When I was small, if there was a girl we liked we would tell a friend to talk to one of her friends. 'He likes her, does she like him?' they would ask.

The first time I dropped a girl was when I was 15 and she was 17. She was getting a bit heavy. She's going out now with a fellow twice my size, so I don't see her much. I liked her, though. When I was working as a mechanic I had a few girlfriends. They're very important when you're with them, but there are more important things.

My main aim in life after all this is to marry and have kids. I'd like to have about eight! I'd also like to be around 30 when I marry. I'd like to live somewhere like Greystones, Co. Wicklow – somewhere that's in the country but not too far from Dublin.

Generally, I like blonde girls, but not peroxide, although I do like fair-haired girls too.

It's weird when you think to yourself that there are girls out there who'd give anything to meet us. I suppose I would feel the same about meeting Sting, or any of my other heroes, but we don't look on ourselves like that.

Sometimes we have to close the curtains at home during the day, as there's a girls' school around the corner and they try to peep in. A lot of them call around at lunchtime and in the evening. They range in age from 13 to about 17. They want autographs and to talk, but sometimes you need your privacy. But it's all part of the job. When we started out, we knew this could happen.

Some bands are rumoured to be gay but I can tell you firmly now that we're not gay. We adore the opposite sex.

BOYZONE
LYNDA
RONAN

MUM'S THE WORD

Noleen Lynch on Shane

Shane is great around the house and helps out when he's here. But for as long as I can remember, he's always been extremely quiet. When he's at home, he plays a lot of music or messes around with motorbikes and cars. Shane didn't really like school – he left at 15 to become a mechanic. On most evenings there can be anything from seven to 40 girls outside. They don't believe me when I say he's not here. But they're great kids.

Marie Keating on Ronan

When Ronan gave up doing his exams to join the band, I was disappointed. But he hated school. It was the last place he wanted to be. We had a lot of conversations among the family and meetings with teachers, and everyone agreed that it was an opportunity he should take.

Now we've got girls hanging around outside all the time. It can become quite annoying when they keep on knocking on the door. But when I first saw Ronan on TV, I thought it was fantastic. He's a very good lad, very caring.

He's not good around the house – you should see the state of his bedroom! But I always know where he is at night and I trust him. Ronan is a worrier and conscientious about what he does, but he hates you to tell him what to do. He's the baby of the family, and I do get lonely when he's away.

Margaret Gately on Steve

I suppose I'm a bit like Stephen's secretary, sorting through his mail every day and telling him what's to be done and where everything is.

It's funny having girls calling to the house all the time. One girl came all the way from Kerry. I felt so sorry for her that I gave her a pair of his jeans, which were ripped. She was delighted, but he went mad when he found out because he liked them.

Stephen's great around the house. If he goes out after promising to do something, he'll say, 'Mam, why did you do that? I could have done it.'

I remember going into a newsagents in Grafton Street one day and seeing a copy of *Smash Hits* on the shelf with Stephen's picture all over the cover. I said to him, 'Buy that for me, I'd like it.' He eventually did, but he was a bit embarrassed about doing it. He's taken me to a couple of concerts with him. I loved Diana Ross.

Pat Duffy on Keith

Keith is extremely sensitive and caring. He's also quite good around the house. He can clean up better than I can, but he's not a good cook. The girls just won't stop coming to the house. On one occasion I went to the front door and told them that I had an awful headache and had to do the dishes, so they offered to do the dishes for me! He's always been playing the drums and used to work out in the gym almost every day.

Sheila Graham on Mikey

Mikey was in hospital from the age of seven weeks until he was seven months, and we nearly lost him. After that, I felt closest to him. We have long chats, and he sends me cards addressed to 'My pal'.

But he does have his moods, and he's very choosy about his food. It can also be really difficult getting him to go to bed. I was delighted when he joined the band – it was something that I would have loved to have done. He often stays in his room, writing songs or listening to music. We are plagued with girls. I had to let two in recently because they were soaking wet from the rain.

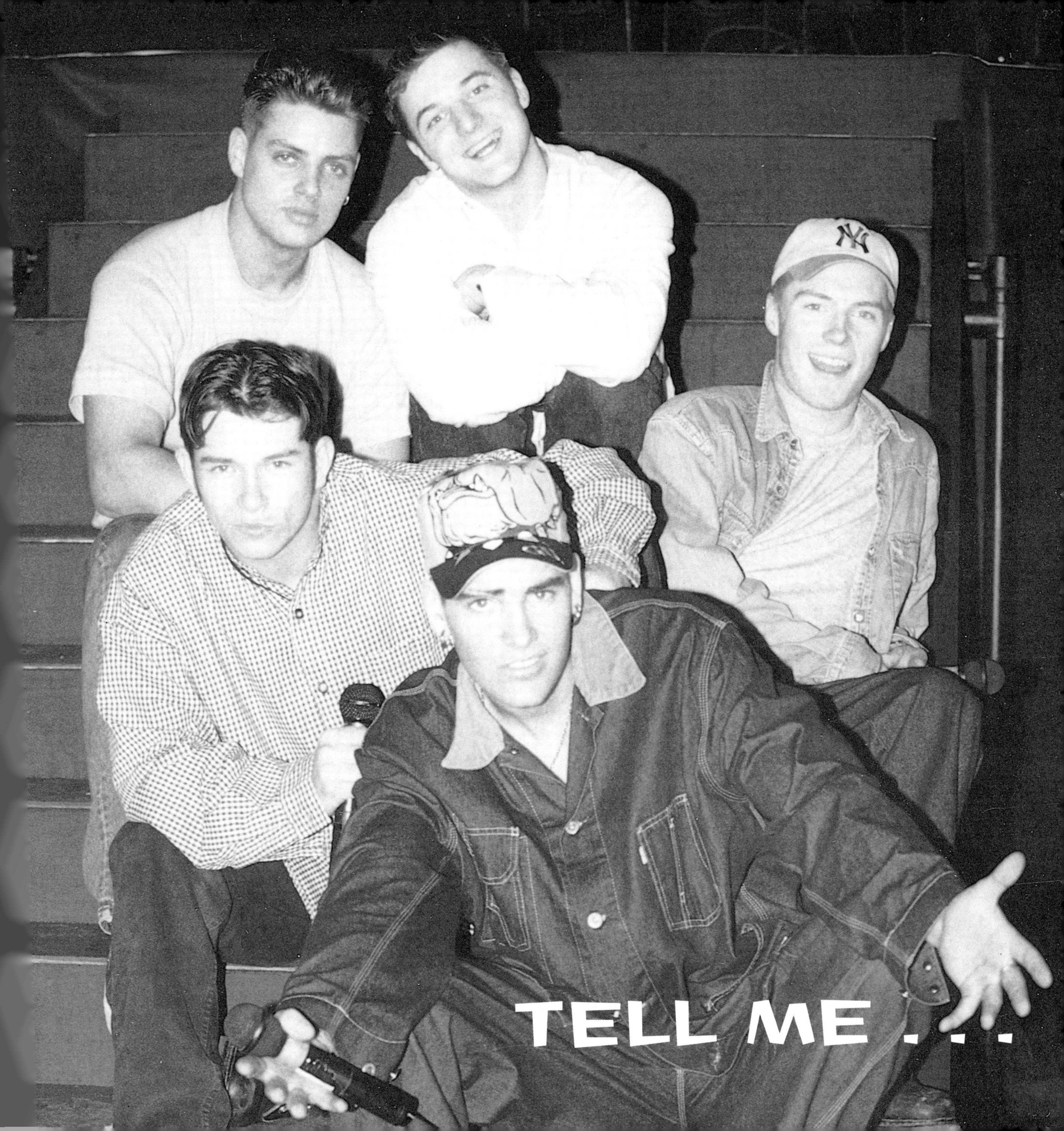

TELL ME . . .

SHANE LYNCH

Place of birth: Dublin
Date of birth: 3.7.1976
Star sign: Cancer
Height: 6′
Weight: 11½ stone
Colour of eyes: blue
Waist size: 30
Shoe size: 9

STEPHEN (STEVE) GATELY

Place of birth: Dublin
Date of birth: 17.3.1976
Star sign: Pisces
Height: 5′ 7″
Weight: 9½ stone
Colour of eyes: blue
Waist size: 30
Shoe size: 7

MICHAEL (MIKEY) GRAHAM

Place of birth: Dublin
Date of birth: 15.8.1972
Star sign: Leo
Height: 5′ 8″
Weight: 10½ stone
Colour of eyes: blue
Waist size: 30
Shoe size: 8

KEITH DUFFY

Place of birth: Dublin
Date of birth: 1.10.1974
Star sign: Libra
Height: 6′ 1″
Weight: 14 stone
Colour of eyes: blue
Waist size: 32
Shoe size: 11

RONAN KEATING

Place of birth: Dublin
Date of birth: 3.3.1977
Star sign: Pisces
Height: 5′ 9″
Weight: 10 stone
Colour of eyes: blue
Waist size: 30/32
Shoe size: 9

If you could be anyone else, who would you be?

All: Nobody. We're happy the way we are.

Would you pose naked for a million pounds?

Mikey: Probably.
Shane: A million quid? You never know!
Others: Definitely not.

What would you like to be doing in ten years' time?

Keith: I'd like still to be in a band that has made it to the top of the pop scene.
Mikey: I'd like to be a successful musician.
Ronan: I want to be in the music business, singing.
Steve: Sitting back, relaxing and enjoying life.
Shane: Probably lying on a beach in Jamaica or somewhere like that.

Do you read all your fan mail?

Steve: Yes, every letter.
Others: Most of it.

Describe your happiest moments.

Keith: The night I got into the band.
Mikey: My 21st birthday.
Ronan: Collecting the National Entertainment Award in Dublin for Best New Act.
Shane: I've always had a nice life.
Steve: Being at home, eating a takeaway and watching some films. Walking through the rain on a dark night.

What do you dream about most?

Keith: Going to the top and being a pop star.
Mikey: Money!
Ronan: Being successful.
Shane: I have really weird dreams, and I can remember them all in the morning.
Steve: I dream about so many different things, it's difficult to say.

Are you superstitious?

Ronan: Yeah, a little bit.
Shane: I'm not superstitious, but I believe in the spiritual world.
Steve: Yes, very superstitious.
Keith and Mikey: Not really.

What do you wear in bed?

Keith: Boxer-shorts or tracksuit legs.
Shane: It depends on who I'm with!
Steve: Boxer-shorts or sometimes nothing.
Mikey and Ronan: Shorts.

Who would you most like to wake up with?

Keith: There are a few girls around the scene I have my eye on!
Mikey: I don't really know.
Ronan: My teddy bear.
Shane: My future wife.
Steve: Whoever I've been going out with.

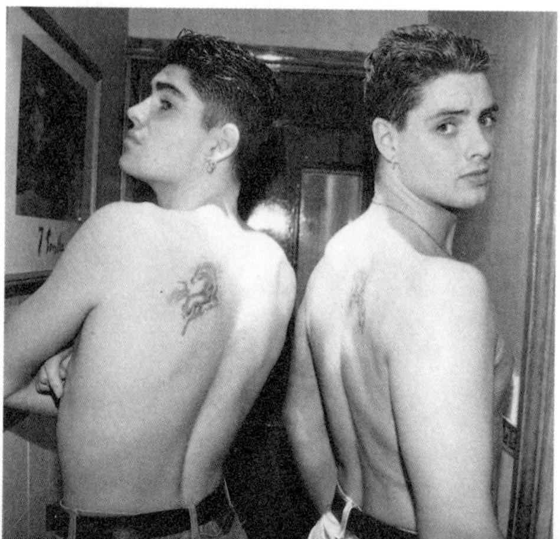

When did you last cry yourself to sleep and why?

Keith: Recently, in a hotel in England when I got depressed.
Mikey: I was about ten.
Ronan: Not long ago. Somebody hurt me.
Shane: It was last year on the *Smash Hits* Roadshow. I had a few beers, was missing home, and got sentimental and very upset.
Steve: Earlier this year. But it's personal.

What's the first thing you notice about a person?

Keith: Their smile, their teeth and their eyes.
Mikey: Their eye movement – whether they can lock their eyes onto yours when they speak to you.
Ronan: Clothes and hair.
Shane: Their height.
Steve: Teeth, eyes, mouth and personality.

What's your favourite chat-up line?

Keith: I don't really have any. If I fancy a girl, I go over and talk to her, I wouldn't chat her up.
Mikey: I don't have one.
Shane: I don't chat up women.
Ronan and Steve: Do you come here often? Ha ha.

What is your favourite part of your body?

Keith: My arms.
Mikey: My stomach.
Ronan: My hair.
Shane: My chest.
Steve: My nose.

What is your favourite film?

Mikey: *Cool Hand Luke.*
Ronan: *State of Grace.*
Steve: *Pretty Woman* or *Sister Act.*
Keith and Shane: *Point Break.*

What is your favourite TV show?

Keith: *Neighbours,* when I get a chance to watch it.
Mikey: *The Cosby Show.*
Ronan: *Quantum Leap.*
Shane: *Top Gear.*
Steve: *Top of the Pops.*

Who is your favourite actress?

Keith: Julia Roberts.
Mikey: Michelle Pfeiffer.
Ronan: I don't really have one.
Shane: Melanie Griffith.
Steve: Whoopi Goldberg or Holly Hunter.

Who is your favourite actor?

Keith: Robert de Niro.
Mikey: Al Pacino, Robert de Niro.
Ronan: Christian Slater.
Shane: Patrick Swayze, Keanu Reeves.
Steve: Tom Cruise, Christian Slater.

Who is your favourite singer?

Keith: R. Kelly or Brian Harvey.
Mikey: Sting.
Ronan: George Michael.
Shane: Bob Marley or Flavor Flav.
Steve: George Michael.

Name your favourite band.

Keith: East 17.
Mikey: The Police.
Ronan: Del Amitri.
Shane: Public Enemy.
Steve: Deuce.

What do you usually do on a Saturday night?

Mikey: Go out.
Ronan: Work.
Steve: I like to stay in and relax.
Keith and Shane: If I'm at home, I go clubbing.

Have you ever shoplifted?

Shane: Yeah, I was only young. It was a bar of chocolate, a Milky Bar, and I didn't get caught.
Others: No.

Name any person, living or dead, you'd like to meet.

Keith: Elvis Presley.
Mikey: My grandparents.
Ronan: River Phoenix.
Shane: Dale Ernhart – he's a racing driver.
Steve: Richard Branson, so I could rob him!

How would you describe yourself in a personal column?

Keith: Big softy who likes fun, has a very loud personality and likes a laugh.
Mikey: Strong, silent type.
Ronan: Quiet, sensitive, paranoid, happy.
Shane: Shy, sensitive to loved ones, fun and very easy going.
Steve: 5' 7", well mannered, fun to be with. I don't know, I've never written one.

What's your reaction to being followed by groupies?

Keith: It's great!
Mikey: It's strange.
Ronan: Amazing, I can't believe it.
Shane: That's my life now, so I don't mind.
Steve: Cool, it's fun. I don't mind, as long as they don't get carried away.

What turns you on?

Keith: A girl sticking her tongue in my ear!
Mikey: Sex!
Ronan: A switch!
Shane: I like girls with long nails to run them through my hair.
Steve: It depends, lots of things.

How far would you go on your first date?

Keith: All the way!
Mikey: Not far.
Ronan: Nowhere.
Shane: I might kiss a girl.
Steve: Not far. I'd probably just kiss. That's it, I wouldn't want to frighten her away.

What irritates you most?

Keith: Greedy people.
Mikey: Probing journalists!
Ronan: People who say 'Wait 'til I give you a laugh'.
Shane and Steve: Smoking.

What's your most prized possession?

Keith: A lighter that my grandfather had in the Second World War.
Mikey: My TV and stereo system and my dog.
Ronan: A grey John Rocha sweater that I love.
Shane: A red stone ring a certain girl gave me.
Steve: Probably my ring or watch, because they were special presents.

How do you know you're in love?

Keith: I suppose you get a funny feeling in your heart.
Mikey: I suppose you just can't wait to see that person again.
Ronan: You just know, you can't explain it. It just happens.
Shane: I don't think words can explain it.
Steve: You would do anything for that person and you care so much for them. Love is so special.

Have you fallen in love recently?

Keith: Yeah, now and again.
Ronan: Yeah.
Others: No.

Would you ever want to be a male model?

Keith: Possibly.
Steve: Yes. I've done some photo work but I'm too small.
Others: No.

Is any part of your body pierced?

Keith: Both my ears are pierced.
Mikey: My left ear.
Ronan: I had my ear pierced, but not any more.
Shane: I've got four earrings.
Steve: No.

Do you have any tattoos?

Keith: I have a black panther on my right shoulder.
Shane: A stallion on my shoulder. I got it done when I was 15, but my Mum didn't find out until I was 18.
Steve: Yes, a Tasmanian devil on my right hip.
Mikey and Ronan: No.

Have you ever been mugged or robbed?

Keith: Yeah, when I was in primary school my bag, coat and money got robbed.
Others: No.

Who's the most famous person you've met?

Keith: Sting.
Mikey: Kylie Minogue.
Ronan: Robbie from Take That, a nice fellow.
Shane: Cilla Black.
Steve: I don't know.

What instruments can you play?

Keith: Drums, bodhran, most percussion instruments.
Mikey: Guitar, bodhran, some drums and a bit of keyboard.
Ronan: Guitar, a little bit of piano.
Shane: Keyboard.
Steve: Piano.

If you were told you had a week to live, what would you do?

Keith: If I had no money, I'd probably rob a bank and live the life of Reilly for a week.
Mikey: Die!
Ronan: Everything that I haven't done so far – parachuting, bungee jumping.
Shane: I really don't know, it'd depend on how much money I had.
Steve: I'd visit everyone I know to say goodbye and that I love them.

What kind of drunk are you?

Mikey: I don't drink.
Others: A happy one.

Do you have any grooming tips?

Keith: Use silkocks base instead of soap.
Mikey: Get plenty of sleep.
Ronan: Drink loads of water.
Shane: Not really, I keep them to myself.
Steve: Yes. Eat healthily.

Have you ever cheated on a girlfriend?

Keith: Yeah.
Others: No.

What type of underwear do you like?

Mikey: Shorts.
Shane: G-strings.
Steve: Calvin Klein or Armani.
Keith and Ronan: Calvin Klein.

Have you ever played spin the bottle?

Keith: Loads of times.
Mikey: Yeah.
Ronan: When I was a kid I did, once or twice.
Shane: Yes, when I was 12 and kissed a girl for the first time.
Steve: Yes, a couple of times when I was a kid.

Have you ever watched a blue movie?

Steve: I'll pass that one.
Keith and Shane: Yes.
Ronan and Mikey: No.

Has your life changed in the last year?

Keith: I can't go to my local anymore. I don't get to see my mates often and can't go clubbing. I get to meet famous people and see the world.
Mikey: It has around me, but I haven't changed.
Ronan: Immensely, totally. You've no social life, you can't go out.
Shane: I've no privacy and no social life.
Steve: In a big way. A big, big way.

Are you a good kisser?

Ronan: I don't know!
Others: Yes.

If a war broke out, would you fight for your country?

Mikey: It would depend on what it was about.
Others: Yes.

Are you still a virgin? If so, why?

Ronan: Yes, I am – I just am, there's no reason.
Others: No.

Do you work out in a gym?

Shane: Yes, mainly bench-pressing and free weights. I don't go into machines, I started when I was 16.
Keith and Ronan: Yes.
Mikey and Steve: Sometimes, just to keep fit.

Are you self-conscious about your appearance?

Mikey: Now and again.
Ronan: To a certain extent you have to be.
Shane: Yes, I pluck my eyebrows and dye my hair.
Keith and Steve: Very much so.

If you weren't in Boyzone, what would you be doing now?

Keith: I'd probably still be in college.
Ronan: Working in my sister's restaurant in New York.
Steve: Probably acting or teaching dancing.
Mikey and Shane: Working as a mechanic.

What's the scariest moment you've had?

Keith: The car crash with Shane last year.
Mikey: In Bulgaria I got swept out too far on a surfboard, but I was able to get back.
Ronan: Splitting my head open an hour before we were due to go on the *Late Late Show*.
Shane: Having to swim from a beach in Portugal after the tide came in.
Steve: Once I woke up and couldn't move my body for a few minutes.

What is your favourite pub/club?

Keith: My favourite pub is the Racecourse, but I can't go there any more. There aren't really any good clubs – the Pod is about the best of them.
Mikey and Ronan: Tamango's (a north Dublin club).
Shane: Coco's (a south Dublin club).
Steve: I can't say, I still want to go there!

What's the best concert you've been to?

Keith: Aerosmith.
Mikey: Boyzone at the Point, Dublin.
Ronan: Take That were great in Dublin and so were East 17.
Shane: Probably UB40.
Steve: The return of the Irish soccer team from the World Cup in 1994 in Dublin's Phoenix Park.

Would you be embarrassed about going on a nudist beach?

Ronan and Steve: Yes, very embarrassed.
Others: No.

Has anyone close to you ever died?

Keith: Plenty of people.
Mikey: My grandparents.
Ronan: My Nanny.
Shane: Yeah, my Nana.
Steve: Yes, my friend Betty.

Which stars have been nicest to you?

Keith: Brian Harvey.
Mikey: Kylie Minogue.
Steve: Kelly from Deuce, Baby from Reel 2 Real, PJ and Duncan.
Ronan and Shane: PJ and Duncan.

What is your favourite method of relaxation?

Keith: Swimming.
Mikey: Meditating a bit.
Ronan: Sleep.
Shane: I like to feel fingernails running through my hair and down my back.
Steve: Sitting down, watching a video.

Are you left or right handed?

Keith and Steve: Left.
Others: Right.

What is your biggest fear?

Keith: Falling off the stage in the middle of a concert.
Mikey: Burning or drowning.
Ronan: Snakes.
Shane: I'm not really afraid of much any more.
Steve: Drowning.

Name your biggest disappointment.

Keith: The length of time it takes to make lots of money!
Mikey: I've had a good few hard knocks.
Ronan: Everything's been great so far.
Shane: The blind date.
Steve: I don't know – it would take hours to find out.

Who is your favourite TV star?

Keith: I don't really have one.
Mikey: Pat Kenny (an Irish chat-show host).
Ronan: Sam Becket from *Quantum Leap*.
Shane: Melanie Griffith.
Steve: Ulrika Jonsson from *Gladiators*.

What is your greatest ambition?

Keith: To go on a Caribbean cruise.
Mikey: To be financially and musically successful.
Ronan: To have a No. 1 album and No. 1 single.
Shane: To become rich.
Steve: To become really big.

Are you an early riser or a night owl?

Keith: I'm a very late riser and I can't stay up late at all.
Ronan: I'm an early riser and I like my sleep.
Shane: I can get up early if I have to and I can stay up until all hours.
Mikey and Steve: Night owl.

What is your favourite colour?

Shane: Black.
Others: Blue.

Do you think you are good looking?

Keith: Well, I'm not ugly.
Mikey: Not really.
Ronan: No, definitely not.
Shane: I suppose I am, yes.
Steve: No, I look in the mirror and say, 'You're ugly'.

If you could change one part of your body, what would it be?

Keith: My feet.
Mikey: My face.
Ronan: My teeth.
Shane: Nothing, I think I'm all right.
Steve: My mouth.

Do you like practical jokes?

Keith: I love them.
Mikey: Yeah.
Shane: Yeah, I often jump out of cupboards and wardrobes.
Ronan and Steve: Yes, except when they're on me.

Do you have smelly feet?

Keith: No, but Mikey does!
Others: No.

Where would you most like to travel in the world?

Keith: South Africa.
Mikey: St Lucia.
Ronan: Paris.
Shane: Hawaii.
Steve: Ireland.

What was the first record you ever bought?

Keith: A compilation album, one of the 'Nows'.
Mikey: The Specials' 'Ghost Town'.
Ronan: Wham's 'Last Christmas'.
Shane: NWA's 'Straight Outta Compton'.
Steve: Sydney Youngblood's 'If Only I Could'.

BOYZONE'S CELEBRITY CITY

Nanci Griffith
(City Centre)

Nick Seymour
(Sth Circular Rd)

Phil Lynott
(Crumlin)

Liam O'Maonlai
(Clonskeagh)

Maria McKee
(Harolds Cross)

Mary Black
(Harolds Cross)

Adam Clayton
(Rathfarnham & Malahide)

Ronan – Boyzone
(Swords & Sutton)

Van Morrison
(Ballsbridge)

Mikey – Boyzone
(Coolock)

Keith – Boyzone
(Donaghmede)

12 
Shane – Boyzone
(Donaghmede)

13 
Bob Geldof
(Blackrock)

14 
Steve – Boyzone
(Seville Place)

15 16 
Larry Mullen
(Howth & Artane)

7 17 
The Edge
(Monkstown & Malahide)

18 
Chris de Burgh
(Dalkey)

18 
Lisa Stansfield
(Dalkey)

19 20 
Bono
(Killiney & Ballymun)

19 
Maire Brennan
(Killiney)

19 

Enya
(Killiney)

19  
Elvis Costello
(Killiney)

ublin is now one of Europe's top music capitals and is the
ise for numerous celebrities in the world of pop and rock.

yzone grew up on the northside of the city with Ronan mov-
g from Sutton to nearby Swords.

2 also came from the northside, but three of them have left
r the southside, except for Larry Mullen who has moved
om Artane to Howth.

ublin is also the base for Irish celebrities such as Chris de
urgh, Enya and Andrew Strong of the Commitments.

on-Irish celebrities who have moved to Dublin include Def
ppard's Joe Elliot, Elvis Costello, Lisa Stansfield, Maria
cKee, Nanci Griffith, Simple Minds' Jim Kerr and wife, Patsy
ensit.

e city's first big international rock star was Thin Lizzy's Phil
nott, who sadly died in 1986.

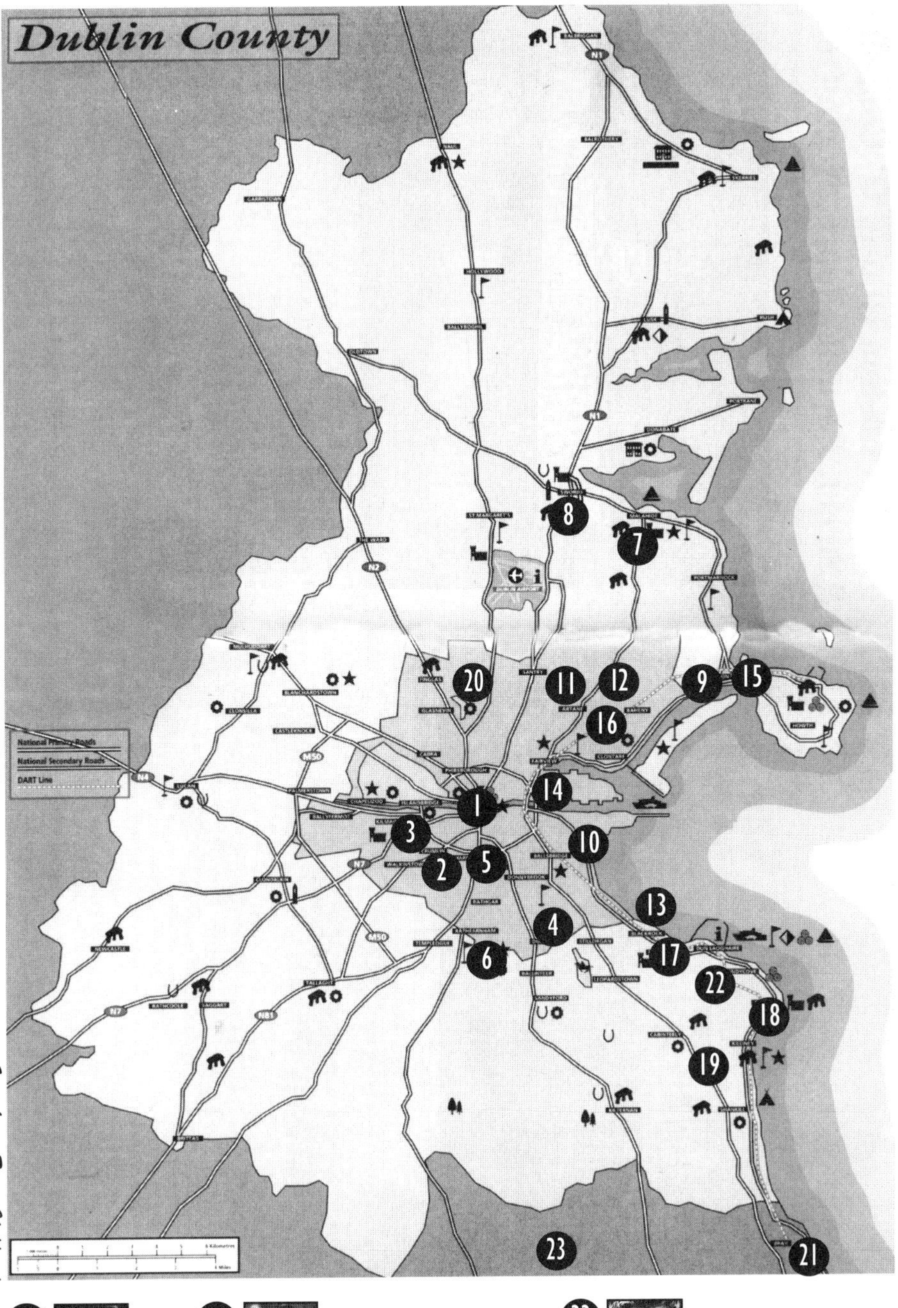

Dublin County

Graphic: Tim Clifford

19 
Jim Kerr
(Killiney)

19 
Patsy Kensit
(Killiney)

21 
Joe Elliot
(Greystones)

22 
Sinead O'Connor
(Glenageary)

23 
Andrew Strong
(Blessington)

LOUIS WALSH - BOYZONE'S CREATOR

I always wanted to form a group like Boyzone, but the time was never right. Eventually, when we had had New Kids on the Block and Take That and there was nothing new in Ireland or the UK, I knew that the time had finally arrived. There was nothing else happening in Irish pop music anyway. There has never been an Irish pop group. It has always been just rock music or traditional music. The closest we ever came to a pop group were the showbands like the Miami.

I am originally from Kiltimagh, Co. Mayo, but I have been living in Dublin since the 1970s. I managed Johnny Logan and Linda Martin, who both won the Eurovision Song Contest. I have also worked as an agent for lots of different acts in Ireland, but a lot of that market had finished, so I had to do something different or else go into a different business.

I got the idea to form Boyzone around September 1993, and we then held the auditions at the Ormond Centre in Dublin that November. We chose six, then two left, and we brought in Mikey, and we were left with the biggest pop group Ireland has ever seen.

I brought in John Reynolds, who owns the Pod nightclub in Dublin, earlier last year as joint manager as I was having a few problems setting up the band and getting them on their feet financially. I was afraid of not being able to keep the thing going, so he came in and we set up the company WAR, Walsh and Reynolds. He looks after the business side of things. I run the show, and that's the way John wants it.

I went to Polygram Ireland and their managing director, Paul Keogh, because I saw that they had spent a lot of money on two Irish acts, the Big Geraniums and Rob Strong. Paul used to promote Budweiser before he went to Polygram, so I was aware that he knew a lot about marketing and that he'd get the record on the shelves and spend money on it. Polygram are the only Irish record company that seem to spend any time and money on their acts.

We spent something like £50,000 on styling and grooming the lads and giving them dance and choreography lessons. Michael Leong did the very first styling, and we sent the pictures around to all the record companies in both Ireland and the UK. Lots of people in the UK – record companies and producers – turned me down. A lot of them didn't even return my phone-calls, I bet they regret it now! Tom Watkins, the East 17 manager, did return my call, though. He liked the pictures. We didn't do business with him but we're on very good terms.

I then brought in Bill Hughes to direct their first video, for 'Working My Way Back To You'. He also did 'Love Me For a Reason'. He's done an incredible job on 'Key To My Life' and I hope he directs all our videos.

I got Ray Hedges in as producer. He worked with Take That and Worlds Apart in their early days, and he did a lot of dance singles too. I was really lucky to get him, as he's given us a lot of advice and direction.

I've also got a really good PR woman, Liz Watson from Sharp End, who helped break them in the UK. I've got a really good team around them.

We did the open-air Beats on the Streets in

Ireland for 2FM Radio, which was really beneficial. But it was the *Smash Hits* Roadshow which made 'Love Me For a Reason' so popular.

I get on really, really well with the lads. The biggest plus is that they get on very well with each other. They're really good friends – there has never been a problem with any of them. I don't worry about them any more. I don't even have to travel with them most of the time.

I think Boyzone can knock Take That off their pedestal. We became the No. 2 act in the UK with just one single. We must remember, though, that if it wasn't for Take That there wouldn't be a Boyzone. I think Gary Barlow is a mega talent. He is Take That, he's absolutely great. People might say that we're an Irish Take That, but they also said that Take That were an English New Kids on the Block when they came out.

I definitely think Boyzone will be a huge name in the UK. We already out-sell Take That by four to one in Ireland. Boyzone will also be massive in Europe and Japan and could even become big in the rest of the world, including America and Australia. Here's hoping!

Acknowledgments

I'd particularly like to thank Louis Walsh for all the help he has given with this book and throughout the years. His partner, John Reynolds, also deserves my acknowledgment. And, of course, I'd like to give a big thank you to all the lads themselves and their lovely families.

I would also like to thank Cathal Dervan for everything he has done on my behalf in bringing this book into being. Mainstream Publishing must also be praised for having the foresight to release the book.

Foremost in my list of thanks are my colleagues at the *Star* newspaper, Dublin, particularly Editor Gerry O'Regan and Paddy Murray, James Dunne and John Donlon. Neil Fraser deserves praise for his wonderful photographs. Other photographers I must thank include Noel Gavin, Martin Maher and Mitchel O'Connor. Also at the *Star* I'd like to thank Olivia, Niamh, Mary, Aisling, Karen, James, Tim, Danny, Niall, Nickie, Alan, Rory, Tom, Jim, Robbie, Connie, Mary and Aenghus. I cannot let this opportunity go without mentioning Derek Cobbe, the man who gave me my break in journalism on the *Longford News* when I was still at St Mel's College.

This book would have been impossible to bring out without the invaluable co-operation of Ailish Toohey of Polygram in Dublin, her boss, Paul Keogh, and their colleagues, Michelle O'Connor, Sharon Dunne and Kevin Fennell. I would also like to thank my friends for putting up with me: Paschal, Rafe, Marilyn, Annette, Barry, Paula, Frank, Shane, Martin, Dessie, John, Sharon, Conor and Killian, among others. Last, but not least, I'd like to thank my family, Jim, Rosaleen, Barry, Sharon and Aoife, for their help and patience. Enjoy the book!

FAN CLUB

The address for the official BOYZONE fan club is:

BOYZONE
PO Box 102
Sanmore
Middlesex
HA7 2PY
ENGLAND